Design For Survival

DESIGN FOR SURVIVAL

New York

★ ★ ★ ★

General THOMAS S. POWER, USAF (Ret.)

with Albert A. Arnhym

Coward-McCann, Inc.

Fourth Impression

Library of Congress Catalog Card Number: 65-15141

MANUFACTURED IN THE UNITED STATES OF AMERICA

When a strong man armed keepeth his palace,
his goods are in peace:

But when a man stronger than he shall come upon him,
and overcome him, he taketh from him all his armour
wherein he trusted, and divideth his spoils.

—LUKE 11:21–22

Contents

Preface

THIS is the second edition of *Design for Survival*. The first edition was never published; it was "banned," as the press put it.

In accordance with military regulations, I had submitted the original manuscript to the Department of Defense in April 1959. The Air Force cleared it with a few minor changes and, in fact, supported its publication. I had no indication of any trouble until, one morning in August 1959, various news media called me and requested my comments regarding a notice in the *Army-Navy-Air Force Journal* which stated that the Secretary of Defense had "banned" the publication of my manuscript.

I immediately contacted the Pentagon to ascertain whether the story was true and, if so, what the reasons were behind the alleged ban. The story proved indeed true, and I learned of the reasons a few days later when Mr. Neil H. McElroy, then Secretary of Defense, invited me to discuss this matter with him. As he explained it, he had denied final clearance of the manuscript solely because he considered it inappropriate for an officer in my position to publish a book pertaining to his area of responsibilities while on active duty.

For a long time thereafter, the "ban" was widely discussed in the public media. I received innumerable expressions of support from persons everywhere, and a Congressional committee initiated a thorough investigation. A prominent senator, who had vigorously opposed the ban both on the floor of the Senate and in public, inserted in the Congressional Record the original Preface of *Design for Survival* as well as a long list of "high-ranking officers in all three services who have published important books while on active duty." But despite all this gratifying support, I made no effort to have the Secretary of Defense change his mind.

I believe very strongly that our democratic form of government, surely the best ever devised by man, takes its strength primarily from three factors which must never be abandoned or impaired. The first factor is the "three-legged stool" principle of government, the three legs being the executive, legislative and judicial branches of government and constituted in such a manner that no one branch can function without the other two. The second factor is freedom of the press so that the public is always fully informed of every aspect of the issues whose final decision must rest with the voters. And the third factor is effective control of the military by the civilian authorities, a basic requirement in a democracy which was recognized and wisely provided for by the founding fathers of this republic.

As the Secretary of Defense had ruled that it was inappropriate to publish my book while I was on active duty, the matter was ended, as far as I was concerned, until I retired. But now that I have put away my uniform, after some 37 years of military service, I consider it appropriate to state my views on the prevention of war.

I realize that this is a risky and perhaps thankless task because, whenever a military man airs his ideas for strengthening the nation's defense effort, he is liable to be called a saber-rattler and warmonger. However, I believe that he can render a greater service to the cause of peace than his detractors. For it is invariably the weak, not the strong, who court aggression and war.

Fortunately, there is a growing awareness among the public that the military problems of survival are no longer the sole concern of the men in uniform and their civilian chiefs. During my tenure as Commander in Chief of the Strategic Air Command I had the opportunity to discuss these problems before literally thousands of people from every walk of life and every section of the country. Despite the diversity of their backgrounds and political convictions, all shared the intense desire to learn more about the threat the nation is facing and what they, individually and collectively, must do to meet that threat.

It was most encouraging to find so much real interest because I maintain that our citizens have not only the right but also the urgent need to know the full truth about the problems that are of such vital importance to them. Indeed, I am more concerned about any attempt to keep unpleasant facts from the people than about their reaction to these facts. It has been my experience that the average American is not easily frightened nor discouraged and that, once he knows what is expected of him, no one and nothing can stop him.

In my discussions, I have endeavored always to present the facts as I knew them, frankly and in terms anyone could understand. To do so on a broader and more inclusive scale is the purpose of this book. It is, therefore, intended neither as a scholarly textbook nor as a vehicle for advancing startling new ideas. It is intended mainly as a report to the nation's stockholders—almost 200 million of them.

To be sure, there is already an extensive and steadily growing literature of more or less authoritative studies on every facet of nuclear strategy and policy. But this book was not written for the military or political scientist; it was written for interested citizens like the untold men and women who came to hear the Strategic Air Command story. It was written for them in the conviction that we cannot solve the problems entailed in our design for survival unless the American people understand these problems and decide to do something about them.

This country has had problems before, and it has always managed to cope with them once it gained the understanding and support of its citizens, for the most powerful force in a democracy is an informed and aroused public. Still, none of the dangers we have faced in the past can compare with the formidable threat of nuclear aggression which we are facing today. Nor will we ever again have the time to plan, to rally and to act after the aggressor has struck. If he were to strike today, he would find us well prepared not only to strike back but to destroy him utterly which has been the main reason why we have managed to deter nuclear aggression to this date. The challenge is to be able to say the same thing tomorrow and throughout the indefinite future. How to meet that challenge in what I consider the most promising and effective way is the subject of this book.

Since I wrote the original manuscript over five years ago, there have been many profound changes in the political, technological and military areas, requiring some updating and revisions. But there has been no change whatever in the fundamental issues involved, namely, the continually growing threat to our survival as a sovereign nation and the problem of insuring a lasting peace which means not only averting general nuclear war but also safeguarding the interests of this country and its allies in "conventional" wars of any type and size.

Nor has there been any change in my conviction that the only hope of achieving our peaceful goals rests in the preservation of credible and flexible military supremacy as an instrument to be wielded by our statesmen with wisdom, discrimination and determination. I realize that this conviction is not shared by a great many citizens who hold opposing opinions. I respect their right to their opinions as I hope they will respect my right to mine. Despite the multitude of conflicting convictions and opinions, I am confident that all of us are striving for the same goal, and that is to maintain peace in this world. Where we differ is in the approach to be chosen in pursuing this goal in the years to come.

While I believe in the preservation of military superiority, others advocate "general and complete" disarmament. There can be no compromise between these two approaches because they are diametrically opposed. I submit that we can no more arm and disarm at the same time than one can dress and undress at the same time. Someone will have to decide which road to choose, and that someone must be no other than the American people. For, in the final analysis, it is they, not the military or the statesmen, who will have to solve the nation's problems.

Palm Springs, California   —THOMAS S. POWER
                                              General, USAF (Ret.)

1. The Lesson of Cuba

THE 12th of October 1962 dawned like any other day for the Strategic Air Command, poised as always to spring into action at a moment's notice.

Alert crews at scores of SAC bases scattered throughout the world were keeping up their around-the-clock vigil, ever ready for the ominous wail of the klaxon that would give them but a few minutes to get their heavily loaded B-47s and B-52s safely in the air.

Somewhere high above the vast expanse of the oceans and wilds of Alaska aerial tankers were refueling SAC bombers to help keep them on airborne alert for as much as 24 hours at a stretch. In thickly cemented blockhouses dug deep into the soil of the Midwestern plains, SAC missile crews maintained their watch, checking again and again to make certain that their "birds" were ready to hurl their deadly cargoes against any aggressor.

And a lone KC-135 jet, carrying a complex array of "black boxes" and manned by a SAC general with his staff of controllers, was flying a wide pattern around Omaha, Nebraska, six miles below, to serve as an invulnerable airborne command post in case a surprise attack should wipe out SAC headquarters and all its alternate headquarters on the ground.

Yes, it was just another day of watch and work for the men of the Strategic Air Command, the most awesome "Big Stick" ever created by man.

I was flying a KC-135 jet tanker back to my headquarters at Offutt Air Force Base, near Omaha, after a routine inspection trip to SAC bases in Europe and Africa, when I received word that I was urgently wanted by my superiors in the Pentagon. Within a few hours, I was closeted with the Secretary of the Air Force who told me of the growing concern about the situation in Cuba. Something had to be done and done fast, and SAC was to be assigned a major role in it. Its first job—photographic reconnaissance over Cuba. The President had to be sure about what was going on in Castro's domain before he could decide on whatever action he might have to take.

What I heard that afternoon in the Pentagon did not come as a surprise to me. In my dual capacity as the Commander in Chief of the Strategic Air Command and Director of the Joint Strategic Target Planning Staff I had to keep myself up-to-date on all available information and intelligence regarding any existing and potential trouble spots in this world. And Cuba was one spot that I had long recognized not only as an ever worsening political problem but also as a mounting threat to the bomber and tanker forces on ground alert at SAC's southern bases.

Nor was the task I had been assigned at the outset of the Cuban crisis anything out of the ordinary for SAC. Its reconnaissance airplanes, loaded with tons of intricate devices, ranged the skies incessantly, gathering all the topographic and electronic intelligence that might be needed by SAC to carry out its retaliatory mission anywhere and any time. In the sprawling underground control center back at Offutt, many highly skilled intelligence experts worked day and night to process, interpret and evaluate the vast amount of data that kept streaming in from SAC's eyes and ears in the skies, augmenting the incessant flow of information emanating from the nation's "intelligence community." Moreover, there was a competent staff of seasoned combat veterans to take care of the operations and planning phases for any type of intelligence mission.

Thus, I needed no detailed explanations and instructions on that fateful October day in Washington, and I lost no time. While still in the airplane heading back to Offutt, I started to put SAC's well-oiled machinery into high gear. On October 14, less than two days after my return, SAC embarked on a grueling schedule of reconnaissance missions high over Cuba. Within a little over a week, SAC aircraft brought back tens of thousands of feet of highly revealing photographs, covering almost every square foot of the enslaved island.

Utilizing all available facilities, the films were processed as rapidly as possible and rushed to Washington. Here sharp-eyed photo interpreters found irrefutable evidence that landscapes, shown peaceful and harmless in photographs taken but a few months earlier, now were dotted with missile sites in various stages of completion.

It was primarily this extensive photographic evidence on which the late President Kennedy based his momentous decision to impose a "quarantine" against Cuba. And it was this staggering proof of the massive buildup of the Soviet missile power at our doorstep which our Ambassador to the United Nations, Adlai Stevenson, exhibited so dramatically in the Security Council.

Photographic reconnaissance was by no means the only contribution of the nation's "Big Stick" during the Cuban crisis. At the request of the Commander in Chief Atlantic, SAC also played a vital part in the sea search for Soviet shipping headed toward Cuba. Its high-flying, long-range aircraft were ideally suited for such a task. When SAC was asked to locate a particular Soviet ship suspected somewhere on the Atlantic, a photograph of that ship with its exact position arrived in Washington a short time later.

But SAC's most important role during those critical days was an indirect one. Indeed, it was mainly the existence of SAC and the instant combat readiness of its powerful strike forces which permitted the President to make his grave decision and accept the risks which his course of action entailed.

No one, perhaps not even Nikita Khrushchev himself, could anticipate what would happen if we would intercept a Soviet blockade runner and try to stop it, if need be by force. If neither the United States nor the Soviets were willing to yield, a direct clash between the two nations was unavoidable. The threat of nuclear war loomed closer than ever before. The President was fully aware of this danger but two vital factors helped him to make up his mind—he had the American people behind him and he could deal from a position of overpowering strength.

That strength, fortunately, also was quite obvious to Mr. Khrushchev. While he kept rattling his missiles, he knew only too well that in any nuclear exchange nothing could stop the Strategic Air Command from dealing his country a devastating and decisive blow. Faced with this grim choice, he had to yield to our demands, and the President's gamble paid off.

But as long as SAC had to serve as the protective "umbrella" under which we conducted our negotiations, we had to make certain that nothing could possibly impair the effectiveness and credibility of that umbrella. Besides, we had to prepare for any contingency, including the ominous prospect of "escalation"— the inadvertent expansion of a local crisis into all-out nuclear war.

The Cuban crisis, like any similar crisis liable to erupt into general war, had one inherent advantage for SAC. It served as "strategic warning" and thereby gave us the time to posture the entire force for immediate action. Normally—if there is such a thing as "normal" during the cold war—some 50 percent of SAC's strike forces was on continuous alert, ready to be launched within the few minutes of warning time we could expect should the Soviets attempt a missile blitzkrieg. But the other 50 percent of SAC's manned forces, just like its missiles, would have to "ride out" the initial onslaught.

With the warning entailed in any major crisis, SAC again had more than the extra few hours it needed to further increase its usual alert status. In one respect, however, the Cuban crisis presented a problem that had been lacking in the previous crises in which SAC had been involved, directly or indirectly. Any missiles fired from Cuba against SAC bases within their reach would permit insufficient, if any, warning to get the ground-alert forces on these bases in the air before they could be destroyed.

Apprised of the President's decision to declare a quarantine against the arms shipments to Cuba, I therefore took a series of preplanned actions designed both to protect the SAC force and to get it ready for any eventuality. Among my first actions was the expansion of the airborne alert, flown by the big eight-jet B-52s, from a small number of training sorties to a sizable percentage of the heavy-bomber fleet.

I had long anticipated the need for an airborne alert which would insure the survival of more heavy bombers in case of a no-warning surprise attack. After much and insistent urging I was finally granted permission to acquire an "on-the-shelf" capability for placing and maintaining a portion of the B-52 fleet on airborne alert "if and when the need should arise." Now this precaution paid off; we could put and indefinitely keep enough B-52s in the air, safe from missiles dispatched from Cuba or anywhere else, to wreak crippling damage on any aggressor. As it turned out, we had to sustain this airborne alert for a full month during which time our B-52s, ready for immediate attack, flew over 20 million miles without a single accident or incident. This unprecedented operation entailed over 2,000 bomber and tanker sorties, requiring almost 50,000 hours of continuous flight.

As SAC's medium bombers, the B-47s, did not lend themselves to sustained airborne alert, they were deployed to previously selected and prepared dispersal bases which included a number of civilian airfields. This dispersal greatly increased the number of targets an aggressor would have to hit simultaneously in order to take the deadly sting out of SAC's counterattack. Moreover, all alert aircraft were evacuated from SAC's exposed southern bases.

Finally, increased alert status was ordered for the entire strike force, including SAC's expanding force of ICBMs—Intercontinental Ballistic Missiles—which were readied for rapid launching. The Command's battle staff was placed on 24-hour duty, and all field commanders were directed to their duty stations. The Strategic Air Command was ready; all it would take to launch salvos of missiles and fleets of bombers, carrying nuclear weapons or conventional bombs, was word from the President.

None of these unmistakable preparations could escape Khrushchev and his military advisers; in fact, it was most important for them to know of SAC's readiness. Of course, it took more than the "Big Stick" to resolve the crisis peacefully but, without it, it could never have been resolved to the advantage of the U.S. For that matter, it is unlikely that the decision to blockade Cuba could have ever been made without the protective "umbrella" of SAC. In President Kennedy's words, ". . . it provided a strategic posture under which the United States forces could operate with relative freedom of action."

The Cuban crisis is a classic example of "dynamic deterrence" in action. Having been intimately connected with that crisis, I saw in it renewed and compelling proof for my contention that it takes a combination of three factors to protect our national interests under all conditions and to maintain peace on *our* terms. The three factors are: credible military superiority along the entire spectrum of modern warfare; courageous and decisive diplomacy; and the active support of the American people.

There could be no doubt about our military superiority and readiness throughout the crucial weeks of the Cuban crisis. Army, Navy and Air Force units were fully prepared to invade Cuba; no one and nothing could have prevented them from taking the island and making short shrift of its Communist rulers. If Khrushchev had chosen to start a nuclear war over the

Cuban issue, SAC bombers and missiles as well as the Navy's Polaris submarines would have implemented their integrated war plan which would have insured the destruction of the Soviet war machine as well as of the entire control and industrial structure supporting it.

Our indisputable military superiority and preparedness provided our statesmen with a powerful tool which permitted them to negotiate from a position of overwhelming strength. President Kennedy made dramatic use of this tool, and the brave actions he took will doubtless be considered by the historians as one of the highlights of his so cruelly ended tenure of the nation's highest office. In so many words, he told Khrushchev to take his missiles out of Cuba or else! Khrushchev, at last, was convinced that the American President meant every word he said and, therefore, did the only thing he could do under the circumstances—he took his missiles back to Russia. Was President Kennedy's diplomacy brinksmanship and playing with fire? Indeed it was, and it was the only kind of diplomacy the Soviets understood. Anything else would have resulted in an ignominious diplomatic defeat for the United States and, worst of all, left Cuba bristling with missiles which would have struck our deterrent posture a serious blow.

But it was not just the military tool that strengthened the President's hand and made it possible for him to take the grave risks entailed in his actions. He also had the full support of an aroused public which had demonstrated its determination to go all the way if necessary for the protection of the nation's interests. To be sure, there were some "Nervous Nellies" who accused the President of risking nuclear war over an issue whose ominous significance they failed to understand. But the vast majority of the American people was solidly behind their President, and it was perhaps that determined attitude of the people more than anything else which convinced Mr. Khrushchev that the next move was up to him—get his missiles out of Cuba or take the consequences, just as President Kennedy had told hi.n.

The public's active support was demonstrated in many ways but, to me, none was more convincing than the reception accorded our B-47 crews which overnight were dispersed to civilian airfields far from their homes and military installations. The crews brought back many heartwarming stories about the enthusiastic and unstinting support they were given by both officials and private citizens. They ranged from the state governor, who immediately furnished troopers to serve as guards, to the little old lady who "adopted" a B-47 detachment and regularly brought the alert crews home-baked cookies and hot coffee. The owner of a motel that was closed for the season opened a whole wing and provided luxurious suites for the crews at a nominal charge. A tobacco growers' association not only made available one of its dormitories for our airmen but also refinished and re-equipped it so as to make it more confortable. The owners of a restaurant closed it to the public on Thanksgiving Day and invited the SAC crews for a big holiday dinner.

The significance of these and many similar stories lies not merely in the fact that men and women everywhere went all-out in assisting our crews in the accomplisment of their mission. Even more significant was this spontaneous demonstration of the people's support of the principles which had brought the B-47s to their airfields. To them, the sleek bombers poised for combat near their homes and places of business did not represent an inviting target for an enemy missile but a visible symbol of the nation's ability and determination to protect the security and freedom of its citizens. That was really what all these people supported.

Thus the Cuban crisis was resolved, at least temporarily, because we had the proper combination of the three vital factors I mentioned earlier—military superiority, courageous diplomacy, and public support. But while the lesson to be drawn from this crisis is unmistakable, I am not completely convinced that we will heed that lesson and make certain that we will have the right combination to meet any future crises. The only ones who can insure that we will always have that combination are the American people themselves, and I am confident that they will do so as long as they understand the nature and scope of the threat to the nation's survival.

But to understand the magnitude of that threat, our citizens must first try to grasp the political and military significance of nuclear weapons and the impact on their lives that has been wrought by the nuclear revolution.

2. Nuclear Revolution

On THE 9th of March 1945, I witnessed the most destructive military attack in the history of warfare—the devastating fire raid on Tokyo.

In that raid, 335 low-flying B-29s dropped some 1,700 tons of fire bombs, causing more physical destruction and loss of life than any other single military action on record. More than fifteen square miles of Tokyo's most densely populated area were burned to the ground; one quarter of all the buildings— nearly 270,000—were destroyed. Almost 125,000 persons were killed or injured; over one million were rendered homeless.

With this raid, we were initiating a new concept of strategic bombing, designed to destroy the Japanese war industry swiftly and thoroughly. The plan called for a series of nighttime strikes against Japan's four principal industrial cities. B-29 four-engine bombers, stripped of their armament, were to carry a maximum load of incendiaries instead of high explosives, and bomb from altitudes averaging only 7,000 feet—less than one quarter of the bombing altitudes flown during previous missions.

This unprecedented and, in the minds of some experts, somewhat risky strategy was employed in the raid against Tokyo for the first time. For this reason, General Curtis E. LeMay, who then headed the 21st Bomber Command, had requested me to observe closely the effects of the entire operation in order to permit definite conclusions as to the feasibility of the new strategy. (The military success of this operation proved to be beyond expectations. In a period of ten days, over 1,500 B-29 sorties delivered almost 10,000 tons of fire bombs against Tokyo, Nagoya, Osaka and Kobe, destroying 31 square miles in the industrial hearts of these cities.)

To obtain as complete a picture as possible for my report to General LeMay, I circled high above the attacking bombers for nearly two hours. I watched block after block go up in flames until the holocaust had spread into a seething, swirling ocean of fire, engulfing the city below for miles in every direction.

True, there is no room for emotions in war. But the destruction I witnessed that night over Tokyo was so overwhelming that it left a tremendous and lasting impression with me.

I had seen destruction before—destruction wrought by large clusters and trains of 500-pound bombs. That, too, had made an impression on me but nothing like the impression created by the Tokyo fire raid. Viewed from six miles up in the sky, exploding 500-pounders look almost insignificant—just little puffs of smoke sprouting from the ground.

As Operations Staff Officer during the atom bomb attacks on Hiroshima and Nagasaki, I did not participate in the actual raids, but shortly after the war I visited what was left of the two cities. This sight, too, was an unforgettable experience, not merely because of the terrible devastation I found but, even more so, because of the incomprehensible fact that such enormous and widespread destruction had, in each instance, been caused by one bomb, dropped from a single airplane. (According to an estimate by the U. S. Strategic Bombing Survey, it would have required 125 B-29s, carrying 1,200 tons of high-explosive bombs, to approximate the damage and casualties at Nagasaki.)

Less than a year later, I was appointed Assistant Deputy Task Force Commander for the Operation Crossroads atom bomb tests at Bikini Atoll and observed the first of a series of atomic explosions. As these explosions increased in power and destructiveness, they kept making an ever greater impression on me.

Then I saw the first explosion of a hydrogen bomb, and everything that I had seen before paled into insignificance.

It is difficult for the average person to appreciate fully the awesome power of the hydrogen bomb, because the mind cannot readily conceive what the eye has not seen. Only those very few who have actually witnessed a nuclear explosion have a fair conception of its unimaginable destructiveness.

Yet all the people in this country, whether or not they have seen a hydrogen bomb explode, must try to grasp the far-reaching implications of this gigantic weapon. They must try to comprehend that it has had a revolutionary impact not only on warfare and international politics but also on every facet of their daily lives. They must try to understand that the hydrogen bomb has created a host of unprecedented problems and that it is vital for them to know what these problems are.

Certainly, almost everyone in this country has heard and read a good deal about hydrogen bombs and seen pictures of nuclear explosions. But what usually impresses people most is the sheer magnitude of this weapon as a tool of war rather than the magnitude of its implications. In the minds of many, a nuclear weapon still is merely another bomb that happens to be more destructive and more dangerous to live with than any weapon of the past.

But the H-bomb is far more than just another weapon with greater destructive power. Nor does its tremendous strategic value stem from its destructive power alone. Of equal importance is the fact that there are now in existence delivery systems which can take the bomb at ever increasing speeds to any target on earth. It is this unparalleled combination of packaged firepower and delivery systems that has revolutionized warfare.

Neither the hydrogen bomb nor any other weapon science may devise can change the fundamental objectives of warfare because these objectives will never change as long as nations resort to force of arms for settling their differences. What has changed, however, are the means and techniques for achieving the objectives of war.

Science and war are strange bedfellows indeed. Somehow, they tend to serve each other's ends, however contrary these ends may be. Throughout history, the desire for superior weapons has helped to stimulate and accelerate scientific progress. Conversely, advances in technology have been responsible for commensurate improvements in the tools of war. The most significant contribution of science in this respect is, undoubtedly, the dramatic reduction in time required to accomplish a military objective.

Offensive forces of the past needed weeks and even months to carry their firepower close enough to their targets to apply it effectively. After extensive preparations, armies together with their weapons and vast stores of supplies had to be moved to the front across many miles of land or sea and then had to fight their way foot by foot across hostile mountains, rivers and heavily defended plains to the enemy's heartlands. The time it took to do all this was reduced to a few hours by the modern jet bomber. The ballistic missile has reduced it to minutes.

Moreover, in the past, after the attacking forces had finally managed to get within reach of a major military objective, it often took them many more weeks and months, if not years, to destroy or capture it. They had to apply their offensive power by shooting myriads of rounds of ammunition out of rifles and guns, by sticking people with a bayonet, or by hitting them over the head with a club. The firepower concentrated in the blockbuster bombs of World War II could achieve the same degree of destruction in far less time. One single hydrogen bomb can accomplish it in a fraction of a second.

This fantastic compression of time is strikingly illustrated by the rapid evolution of strategic airpower since World War I. After the United States entered that war, it took American air squadrons a full year to reach the point where they could support the ground forces at the front. Consequently, elements of the U. S. Air Service were in combat for only seven months—

from April to November 1918. During that period, they made about 150 bombing raids, the deepest 160 miles into enemy territory. The total of bombs dropped amounted to 138 tons. The greatest air action in this war entailed approximately 360 airplanes which dropped some 70 tons of explosives on railroad yards.

By the end of World War II—less than thirty years later— strategic bombing had developed from a relatively minor support activity to the principal offensive operation. Laying waste 125 large cities and disrupting the entire economy of two powerful nations, it was strategic bombing more than any other factor that, ultimately, forced the unconditional surrender of Germany and Japan.

The combat record of the air forces of the Western Allies during World War II reads like statistics from an astronomy text. In the European Theater alone, the allied air forces, with a peak of almost 28,000 combat planes and 1,335,000 men assigned to combat commands, flew more than 1,440,000 bomber sorties, in addition to 2,680,000 fighter missions. Almost 2,700,-000 tons of bombs were dropped, over half that amount on Germany proper, destroying or heavily damaging an estimated 3,600,000 dwellings, killing more than 300,000 persons and injuring 780,000. In the raid on the industrial city of Dortmund on March 12, 1945, over 1,100 airplanes dropped nearly 5,000 tons of explosives. Berlin was hit by a total of 77,000 tons of bombs which reportedly destroyed one-fifth of its built-up area.

More than 650,000 tons of bombs were expended in the Pacific Theater, most of them by B-29s which had accumulated a total of 90 million air miles by V-J Day. Although the bomb tonnage dropped by the B-29s on the home islands of Japan was only a fraction of that expended against Germany, the U. S. Strategic Bombing Survey concluded that the damage was practically equivalent. Nine months of B-29 raids resulted in a total of over 800,000 civilian casualties and the almost complete annihilation of Japan's war industries.

Then, on August 6, 1945, a lone B-29 bomber, the *Enola Gay,* initiated a new era in warfare when it dropped the first atomic bomb on Hiroshima, destroying a city larger than Fort Worth. The second and only other atom bomb used in war hit Nagasaki on August 8. Six days later, World War II was over.

The military contribution of the two atom bombs actually was a minor one. In fact, conventional bombs had done such a thorough job of destruction in Japan that no targets would have been left for the atom bombs if the 21st Bomber Command had not been directed to save four cities, including Hiroshima and Nagasaki, for that purpose. The principal value of the two atom-bomb attacks lay in wiping out what little will to continue the hopeless battle was left in the Japanese people and thus speeding their unconditional surrender. It was the devastating effect of systematic strategic bombing that forced this powerful and well-disciplined nation to sue for peace, eliminating the need for a lengthy and costly invasion operation that might have cost us a million or more casualties.

But despite the worldwide devastation of hundreds of major population and industrial centers and despite tens of millions of military and civilian casualties, most of the nations involved in World War II—victors and vanquished alike—were able to stage a remarkable recovery. From the very moment hostilities ceased, the ugly scars of war began to disappear at an ever accelerating pace. Cities which seemed hurt so badly that it would take decades to rebuild them rose from the ashes more beautiful and modern than before. Factories reduced to rubble went back into operation with what little machinery could be salvaged and, in many instances, soon managed to produce more than they did before the war.

A typical example of the world's amazing recovery from the deep wounds of World War II is the city of Hamburg, West Germany's chief port. An important strategic target, Hamburg was hit by a series of raids during July and August 1943 which were among the most devastating of the war. It received a total of 22,500 tons of bombs, raining down at a rate as high as 50 tons per minute. As a result of the raids, 6,200 acres were bombed into ruins; 48 percent of all dwellings were destroyed; over 60,000 people were killed. Yet, five months later,

Hamburg had regained 80 percent of its former productivity. Less than ten years after the war's end, its degree of recovery easily matched that of the rest of West Germany, whose production rate was already over 150 percent greater than it had been in 1936.

Such rapid and effective recovery would be impossible after an all-out nuclear war. Casualties would be so vast, destruction so thorough and widespread, and lingering radioactivity so prohibitive that the recovery effort would be impeded seriously and take many more years than it did after World War II. The full magnitude and scope of this threat could not be anticipated in the early days of the nuclear revolution. Nevertheless, the destruction and casualties caused by the two atom bombs dropped on Japan were so overwhelming that they set off a chain reaction of important and far-reaching changes in many areas.

Military strategists, who had just learned to plan in terms of huge bomber formations, had to revise their thinking completely and learn to plan in terms of a few aircraft possessing destructive capability of unprecedented proportions. Statesmen and diplomats all over the globe had to reassess their foreign policies because of their countries' sudden military obsolescence and vulnerability to atomic attacks.

Most importantly, the United States, with a seemingly safe monopoly in atomic weapons for some time to come and the means to carry these weapons to distant targets, had emerged as the world's greatest military power. But despite its unchallenged military supremacy, the United States posed no threat to the newly gained peace. Conversely, we could feel secure from aggression because the Strategic Air Command, established in March 1946, had the unquestioned ability to destroy any nation foolhardy enough to attack us.

Today, we no longer possess an atomic monopoly nor the security that this monopoly provided. While the spectacular advances in nuclear weapons and ballistic missiles have improved our offensive strength tremendously, they have also given the Soviets the means to undertake what Lenin and Stalin never

thought possible—a massive attack on the United States mainland. Our vulnerability to such an attack is, from our point of
view, the most significant effect of the nuclear revolution. We
must, therefore, ask ourselves exactly what this unprecedented
threat to our physical security entails.

No hydrogen bomb has ever been dropped in wartime, but
this much we have learned from testing it—the bomb is so un-
believably powerful that, in comparison, the atom bombs
loosed on Hiroshima and Nagasaki seem like mere firecrackers.
All the bombs dropped by the Allies during World War II,
both in the European and Pacific Theaters, totaled about 3,350,-
000 tons. In modern nuclear parlance, this figure is expressed as
3.35 megatons, which is less than the yield of one medium-sized
hydrogen bomb or missile warhead.

It would have taken *millions* of B-17 Flying Fortresses of
World War II fame to carry a load of conventional bombs that
would match the explosive power of a single multi-megaton
nuclear weapon. To get an idea of what this means, let us sup-
pose that one such weapon had impacted near the center of a
metropolis.

The exploding weapon has created a crater about 350 feet
deep and some 3,700 feet in diameter. Beyond this enormous
crater, a "lip" of radioactive debris extends outward for approximately 1,800 feet and to a height of 85 feet—enough to cover a
six-story house.

The resulting fireball would be about four miles in
diameter, and temperatures within that fireball would probably
be around 8,000 degrees Fahrenheit. All matter within that
area—animate and inanimate—has been pulverized. And lingering radioactivity would make it impossible to rebuild this area,
at least within our lifetime.

Large buildings as much as six miles from the impact point
would now be nothing more than ripped-out shells of rubble
and collapsing roofs and walls. In addition to the blast effects
which have caused this damage, the intensive heat has sparked
numerous big fires, and many more fires have resulted from
broken gas lines, electrical short circuits and secondary explo-

sions. Widespread devastation, raging fires, and casualties in the millions extend to about 18 miles from the impact point.

Heavy radioactive fallout would start raining down on this area within twenty minutes after detonation and would last for approximately half an hour before subsiding. Radiation would prevent anyone from entering this area for the next 10 hours at least. And for 48 hours after time of burst, a lethal fallout pattern about 18 miles wide would extend downwind to a distance of some 130 miles, resulting in additional heavy casualties.

All this would be caused by one single nuclear weapon, according to estimates published by the Atomic Energy Commission. These figures may vary with the size of the weapon but are indicative of what we would have to expect if we should ever be subjected to a nuclear surprise attack. Too many people in this country fail to understand the ominous implications of such an attack, possibly because they still think in terms of the surprise attack on Pearl Harbor which, eventually, led to the defeat of the aggressor, not of the United States.

The attack on Pearl Harbor was successful beyond the aggressor's expectations. Our defenses, caught unawares, were ineffectual; the damage was great. However, the losses we suffered did not affect our real strength because the strength of this country did not lie in Pearl Harbor; it lay in its industry and in its people. The principal effect which the Pearl Harbor attack had on the United States was to arouse its citizens into action. They rolled up their sleeves and, in the months and years to follow, built up the best-equipped and best-trained military force in history.

If an aggressor were similarly successful today in launching a surprise attack against us with bombers and missiles carrying nuclear weapons, he would hurt us, and hurt us badly. In addition to enormous destruction and casualties, much of our military force-in-being would be destroyed. There would be no time to mobilize our resources; there would be no time to rebuild our military machine so as to turn initial defeat into ultimate victory, as we managed to do after Pearl Harbor.

Modern weapons, therefore, encourage aggression because

they offer invaluable advantages to those who are equipped—
and unscrupulous enough—to attain their ends through a nuclear blitzkrieg. For the aggressor can strike with little or no
warning at all and, conceivably, exact such a heavy toll as to
gain a decisive victory in his initial attack. The Soviets are
acutely aware of these advantages; in fact, their military writers
have made no secret of the great importance they place on the
element of surprise in a nuclear war. For this reason, we would
be courting disaster if we were to relax our defensive posture in
the expectation that there would be sufficient warning of an
impending attack to give us time to prepare for it.

Military strategy deals with two types of warning—"strategic
warning" and "tactical warning." Expressed in the simplest
terms, "strategic warning" is of such duration as to give the
field commander enough time to move into fighting position
and configuration. "Tactical warning" is of such short duration
that the field commander must fight in whatever position and
configuration he happens to be at the time the enemy strikes.

I maintain that we received strategic warning of the Communists' intentions as early as 1848—over one hundred years ago—
when Karl Marx and Friedrich Engels published their *Communist Manifesto*. Since then, the Communists have told the world
in millions of spoken and written words what their goals are.
They have proved in countless brutal actions—in Finland, Poland, Korea, Hungary—that they are determined to achieve
these goals by any means at their disposal.

Whatever qualities we may ascribe to the Soviets, we certainly cannot accuse them of hiding their intentions—to impose Communist dictatorship on the nations of the world, if
need be by force of arms. So long as the United States stands in
the way of the Soviets' ultimate goal, it must remain on guard
against the grim fate suffered by other nations that had resisted
submission to Communist rule. The knowledge of this danger
is adequate *strategic* warning of a possible attack.

The main concern, therefore, is sufficient *tactical* warning of
an actual attack. This has become one of the most critical problems of the nuclear era because of the fantastic reduction in

warning time engendered by modern weapons and delivery systems. In the past, it was not possible for nations to hide extensive preparations for waging an aggressive war. Calling up of reserves, unusual troop or ship movements, intensified border activity and similar preparations were normally conspicuous enough to serve as adequate warning signals and give the intended victim time to build up his defenses. It is true that history abounds in cases where such convenient and timely warning was not heeded, usually with disastrous results. These cases in no way detract from the value of strategic warning but merely demonstrate how its advantages can be nullified by political or military negligence.

I happened to be stationed in the Philippines in 1937 when the U. S. river gunboat *Panay* was attacked by Japanese bombers near Nanking and sank with a loss of 2 men killed and 30 wounded. Most of us near the scene were certain that this meant war, and American military units in the area were readied for action. We were surprised when this incident was resolved peacefully, with the American government readily accepting Japanese explanations and apologies. What surprised us was the gullibility of our statesmen who failed or did not care to recognize the unmistakable warning of impending war with Japan.

The unprovoked bombing of American and British shipping was not a solitary incident, as it was apparently made out to be back home. It was one of a long series of incidents and actions which made it clear that the Japanese war lords were determined to expand their aggression on China into war with the Western powers. I had the opportunity to visit China and Japan during my service in the Philippines, from 1936 to 1938, and only a fool or a blind man could have failed to notice Japan's extensive preparations for a major war. Even the Japanese living in the Philippines assumed a high-handed and intransigent attitude which demonstrated convincingly that they considered our days in the Far East numbered.

After my return to the States in 1938, I discussed my observations and conclusions at every opportunity but found nothing but disbelief and disinterest. Many people had not even heard of the Philippines or knew where they were located, and even those who did know could not be made to understand the ominous implications of the trouble that was brewing in that remote corner of the world. Finally my wife said to me, "Why don't you give up? They don't understand what you're talking about." She was right, and I stopped trying to convince people that Japan was preparing for war against us.

Of course, I was only a junior officer then, but there were many others in more prominent positions who knew or should have known far better than I did that the men in power in Japan at that time would not stop with the conquest of China; their vast preparations could mean only one thing—war with the United States. Had we heeded this unmistakable strategic warning, we would have been far better prepared when the Japanese did strike at Pearl Harbor and might have saved untold thousands of American lives. The war in the Pacific might have been shortened considerably and, conceivably, been averted altogether.

But all this is history, and the strictly military type of strategic warning that I observed in the Far East has yielded to political and related indicators. Today, preparations for large-scale aggression no longer entail suspicious and extensive movements of ground troops or warships. The initial and, possibly, decisive phase of a nuclear war can be initiated from any convenient and desired location—missile-launching sites and air bases thousands of miles from their intended targets or missile-equipped submarines and aircraft carriers far out at sea. Indeed, modern weapons have ushered in the era of "long-distance wars," wars that can be carried on from the home bases of countries half a world apart.

Therefore, the only conclusive warning we could expect to get in case of nuclear aggression would be "tactical warning," that is, warning that swarms of hostile missiles have been launched against us and will impact in the United States within a matter of minutes. This warning would come from our "Ballistic Missile Early Warning System" and would amount to some twenty minutes at best. But even the optimum tactical warning we could hope for—about thirty minutes if we could detect a hostile missile salvo from Russia immediately upon launch—would be of no value unless we were fully prepared at all times to react effectively within that short period. This pertains not only to the capability of our strike forces to counter aggression instantly and decisively but also to their survivability in the face of a massive surprise attack.

The problems resulting from the drastic reduction in warning time are aggravated by the fact that modern weapons have placed a far greater premium on the initiative than ever before, giving the aggressor an added advantage which, again, is not well understood. If we had, for instance, twice as many bombs and twice as many missiles as the Soviets, most people in this country would feel secure from aggression. Such reasoning, however, does not take into account the large degradation of the defender's military strength if he is subjected to a surprise attack.

The nation which takes the initiative in starting a war can select the most favorable conditions, time and strategy for its attack and then commit its entire striking force to action. The nation to be attacked, however, cannot possibly maintain its entire striking force on full alert status for an indefinite period of time but must man the alert positions in shifts. The shift on duty at any one time represents only a fraction of the defender's forces, and it is merely that fraction which would be ready for instantaneous action whenever and wherever the enemy should decide to strike. Because of the rapidity and severity of the opening blow in a nuclear war, the rest of the defender's forces —that is, those not on alert duty—cannot be counted upon in the initial and most important battle, and for that matter, may not see any action at all.

Hence, the concept of "nuclear parity" is grossly misleading because a nation's military strength can no longer be measured in terms of quantity and quality alone. With all other factors being equal, the nation which takes the initiative in nuclear war automatically assumes military superiority.

Modern weapons thus have made aggression a most attractive venture for nations bent on conquest, but they have also raised its price to unprecedented proportions. No matter how successful his surprise attack, the aggressor cannot escape some measure of retaliation, and every hydrogen bomb dropped on his soil may mean the loss of one large city and of untold thousands of his people. If he weighs the profits he hopes to gain from aggression against the possible costs, he may find that the stakes in nuclear war are far too high to warrant the gamble. And that is the basic reasoning behind the principle of deterrence through superior military strength.

But it will take more than the plaintive voice of reason to save the world from the holocaust of a nuclear war. As Lecomte du Noüy wrote in *Human Destiny*: "For the first time in the history of man, the conflict between pure intelligence and moral values has become a matter of life and death. All we can do is hope that humanity will profit by this lesson. Alas, we doubt it."

I doubt it, too. There can be no assurance of peace on earth so long as any nation is governed by men to whom the beguiling promises of the nuclear revolution mean more than the voices of reason and conscience.

3. The Communist Threat

THE common citizens of Soviet Russia still have little opportunity to tell the outside world exactly how and what they feel. But of this I am firmly convinced—the Russian people do not want war.

They want war as little as the American people or the British people or any other people in this world. Yet, I am just as firmly convinced that the threat of nuclear war, sparked by Communist aggression, is very real and that it is, in fact, growing rather than diminishing as some people like to believe.

These seemingly contradictory convictions are supported by the same reasons, namely, the contradictory characteristics of the Russian nation. It is difficult to appreciate the gravity of the Communist threat without first gaining an understanding of these characteristics.

There is a great deal of truth in Paul Winterton's often quoted plaint that ". . . there are no experts on Russia—only varying degrees of ignorance." This, however, should not imply that we, as a nation, are pitiably ignorant about what is going on in Russia. We probably know more about Russia than most people assume, but we make less use of our knowledge than most people think.

I had the opportunity to visit the Soviet Union myself when

I accompanied General Nathan F. Twining, then Chief of Staff of the U. S. Air Force, on his trip to that country in June, 1956. General Twining had been invited to attend the air show at Tushino Airport, near Moscow, on the occasion of Soviet Air Force Day. Following this, General Twining and his party were to visit what were described as "several technical air installations" as well as a "higher training establishment" of the Soviet Air Force.

After careful consideration of all factors involved, President Eisenhower granted permission to accept the invitation. While our visit was brief—only eight days—it was so crowded with tours and special events for us that we undoubtedly saw and heard more in this short period of time than almost anyone else could hope to learn in weeks or months, if at all.

Actually, we learned little that we did not already know. In fact, it was suggested that we could draw more interesting conclusions from what we were *not* shown than from what we did see. But whatever we saw during our tours and whatever we heard in our informal although guarded talks with political, military and industrial leaders helped to confirm what many of us had suspected for some time. The rate of progress and improvement in Soviet aerial weapons, backed by a massive scientific and industrial effort, was far greater than most Americans believed possible.

There could no longer be any doubt in our minds that the Soviets were rapidly reaching the point where they could successfully challenge our technological superiority. It was equally obvious that the principal objective of their technological effort was to build up a formidable war machine even though our hosts went to great lengths to emphasize the defensive nature of the equipment that we were shown.

As for my personal impressions, I realized, of course, that my brief experience, however enlightening, was too superficial and inconclusive to markedly improve my "degree of ignorance," let alone make me an expert on Soviet military affairs. However, my visit served to lend depth and substance to various theories I had formulated on the basis of what I had learned previously about the Communist system and its threat to the Free World. Moreover, I met some of the key men behind the global Communist conspiracy, both formally and informally, and I was struck with both their cocky self-assurance and brutal frankness. Most of all, I experienced what it meant to live in an absolute police state and to have supreme power concentrated in the hands of a very few.

But the visit to Russia gave me far more than some general impressions. It made it possible for me to view subsequent events and information in a better light and, on that basis, arrive at certain conclusions which I consider to be well supported. Much has happened since that visit some years ago, and there have been many changes. But the nature and gravity of the Communist threat have not changed nor have my conclusions. In fact, I am more convinced than ever that the threat continues to mount while many people seem inclined to believe that the exact opposite is true. The most frequently cited reasons for such optimism include the ideological and political differences in the Communist camp, the economic problems in Soviet Russia, and the "nuclear stalemate." I do not share this optimism nor do I accept any of the reasons advanced for it.

My conclusions concerning the Communist threat today can be summarized briefly as follows:

1. The Soviet leadership is irrevocably committed to the achievement of the ultimate Communist objective, which is annihilation of the capitalist system and establishment of Communist dictatorship over all nations of the world.

2. The Soviets realize that they cannot achieve their ultimate objective unless and until they succeed in eliminating the major hurdle in their path, the United States. They are determined to resort to any means at their disposal in order to remove that hurdle.

3. Soviet propaganda endeavors to disguise the struggle between the Western and Communist worlds as a conflict of opposing ideologies which permit of peaceful coexistence, threatened only by the "selfish warmongering of the American imperialists." Purpose of this and similar propaganda tactics as

well as of other Soviet cold-war techniques is to alienate our allies and to weaken us politically, militarily, economically and morally.

4. Any pacts and agreements with the Soviets can be expected to be as meaningless and one-sided in the future as they have been in the past. Instruments of this kind are a favorite Soviet device to make their intended victims relax their guard and, therefore, tend to increase rather than decrease the threat of aggression. This applies, in particular, to proposed disarmament and similar agreements designed to weaken our deterrent posture.

5. The Soviets endeavor to attain their ends without getting involved in a nuclear war, even if they were certain of winning it. The reason is not only the price they would have to pay for what, at best, would be a Pyrrhic victory, but also the economic demands of the arms race and the growing competition with China for undisputed leadership in the Communist world of tomorrow. Therefore, the Soviets will continue to pursue a combination of limited-war and cold-war tactics expected to destroy our democracy as effectively as successful nuclear aggression ever would, and at far less risk and cost to them. This objective is being furthered by some influential American citizens who, in their ardent desire for peace at any cost, play into the hands of the Soviets by promoting unilateral disarmament, one-world government and surrender of our national sovereignty.

6. If the Soviets should become convinced that they cannot subdue the United States through their present strategy, they will have no choice but to resort to all-out military action and they have long prepared for such a contingency. As the Soviets would not deliberately precipitate a general war unless they believed the odds to be heavily in their favor, they set out to achieve military superiority to such a degree that, whenever necessary, they could attack us successfully and at acceptable losses to themselves.

7. The experiences of World War II proved to the Soviets that they could never hope to attain military superiority over the United States without first attaining technological superi-

ority. For this reason, they embarked on an unparalleled, long-range effort to wrest technological leadership from this country. As a result, we are now in a close race with the Soviets for overall supremacy on the ground, in the air and in space. We will have to accelerate our pace considerably if we are to maintain our lead in that race and thereby preserve not only our deterrent against aggression but also our capability to resist nuclear blackmail.

8. Because of their nuclear weapons and modern delivery systems, especially missiles, the Soviets now have the capability to launch a surprise attack on the United States. They appear confident that, with continued advances in their weapon systems, especially those operating in or from space, such an attack can gain them a quick, decisive and none-too-costly victory, leaving the Eurasian complex at the mercy of their powerful ground forces. If we permit the Soviets' offensive and defensive capabilities to grow at a faster rate than ours, the threat of aggression will grow commensurately.

9. Although the Russian people do not want war, they would undoubtedly support their leaders in a war against the United States. It does not appear likely that the steady rise in the overall educational level or contacts with the West will basically change the attitude of the Russian people and, eventually, turn them against their rulers.

10. Despite the ever growing threat of nuclear war, we should be able to maintain peace on our terms if we pursue a realistic and dynamic policy of deterrence against any and all potential aggressors, including Red China. There still remains the possibility, however, that a general war may develop because of an accident, miscalculation or escalation of a local conflict, and we must be prepared for such a contingency.

In this and subsequent chapters I shall elaborate on these conclusions and endeavor to show that they are based on facts, not personal opinion. I consider a thorough discussion necessary because I appreciate that many people in this country will not concur in some—or any—of my conclusions.

They may disagree, not necessarily because they are Communist sympathizers or pacifists, unrealistic or uninformed, wishful thinkers or professional optimists, but perhaps because, like most of us, they are inclined to judge others by their own standards of living, values and morals. Thinking in terms of our exceptionally high standards of performance and principles can easily lead to a dangerous underestimation of the performance and principles of other peoples.

The greatest mistake we can make in this respect is to underestimate the Soviets' intentions and their determination as well as their capability to pursue these intentions. The last time we made such a mistake, we had to pay for it so dearly that it should have taught us a lasting lesson. In his book *Mein Kampf,* Adolf Hitler told us exactly what he intended to do and how he would do it. Most people in the democracies, however, paid little attention to what they believed to be the harmless rantings of a diseased mind. It took World War II to prove them wrong.

The Soviets, too, have told us—and are still telling us—what they intend to do and how they expect to go about it. So far, they have done a good job of putting into practice what they have been preaching. There may well be disagreement on the gravity of the Communist threat, but there cannot be any disagreement on the facts in the record. For the record shows that the Communists are now controlling almost one-third of the population of the world—over 900 million people—and about one quarter of its geography.

I should consider this as rather convincing proof that the Soviets are as firmly determined and committed to pursue their widely publicized intentions as Hitler ever was. In view of their past record it would, therefore, be fatal complacency to assume that anyone or anything could make the Soviet rulers abandon their announced intention to gain control of the rest of the world's people and geography.

The United States has been and still is the major bulwark against the Communist avalanche in the Free World. Unless Communism succeeds in shattering that bulwark, its very nature would condemn it to slow but certain deterioration. Like an avalanche, an aggressive and expansionist ideology such as Communism cannot afford to stop or be stopped anywhere on its path. The immense strength of the United States and its inexorable determination to resist Communist domination have, therefore, created a difficult dilemma for the Soviets. Their problem is that a reputedly irresistible force—Communism—is up against an immovable object—the United States.

Although this problem has existed ever since the objectives of modern Communism were formulated by Lenin, the Soviets made no concerted effort to resolve it until after World War II. Despite the huge losses they suffered in this war, their alliance with the victorious powers paid off handsomely with respect to territorial gains, giving them an auspicious start on the long road to global conquest. Our avowed opposition to further Communist expansion, backed by our atomic monopoly, loomed as the only major obstacle on that road. The Soviets, therefore, concluded that the time had come to tackle the American problem in earnest.

Military action against the United States was, of course, out of the question in those early postwar years. Any attack on the American forces in Europe and those of its Western allies would have had disastrous consequences for the Communists. Due to its technological and industrial superiority, the United States had attained such overpowering military strength that no country, least of all industrially backward Russia, was in any position to challenge it.

The American example demonstrated the tremendous importance of technology in modern warfare. The Soviets decided to follow this example and forthwith concentrated their efforts on the rapid but carefully planned buildup of a modern war machine designed to surpass eventually that of the United States. Nothing was overlooked that could serve to expedite this ambitious program. Years of scientific work were saved by the effective utilization of captured German scientists and by obtaining extensive data on American technology through a huge and ingenious intelligence system.

Vast new research and development centers were created in record time, supplemented by swiftly expanding industrial facilities for the mass production of advanced military matériel. To ensure a continuous and adequate supply of scientists and engineers, the Soviets initiated what soon became the most elaborate and productive educational program of its kind in the world.

Because of this unparalleled program, the quantity and quality of college graduates in Russia, especially in the engineering and related sciences, increased steadily, in contrast to those in most countries of the Free World. Large numbers of Russian youth were induced to choose engineering or allied careers, through "selective compulsion" if necessary, but mainly through early indoctrination and appealing incentives, such as liberal stipends, awards and bonuses, and the prospect of professional prestige and social position.

In addition, the Soviets established an advanced educational system for improving the technical qualifications of their military personnel. The scope and thoroughness of this system were impressed on me when I inspected the famous Zhukovskii Air Engineering Academy in Moscow during my trip to Russia in 1956. We learned that this academy had some 2,500 students— all Air Force officers, ranking from first lieutenant to major— who underwent a five-year course of considerable breadth and depth. The high quality of the instructors and the equipment available for training were most impressive. Also, it was significant that the Soviets could spare so many Air Force officers, outstanding enough to be selected for this academy, for such a long period of time. And this was only one of a number of technical schools of similar quality and scope.

In all likelihood, the Soviets did not contemplate an actual attack on the United States when they first started the modernization and buildup of their military machine. Military action was planned initially for the conquest of the Eurasian complex while increasing isolation and the stepped-up cold war, coupled with Soviet-directed subversive activities, were expected gradually to lead this country into the Communist camp.

Lenin, the father of modern Communism, reportedly summarized Soviet strategy in the following words: "First we will take Eastern Europe, then the masses of Asia, then we will encircle the United States which will be the last bastion of capitalism. We will not have to attack. It will fall like an overripe fruit into our hands." Whether or not Lenin actually used these words, this was his strategy and it remained unchanged until the Soviets came into possession of the hydrogen bomb.

Strangely enough, the Soviets did not fully recognize the unique advantages offered by nuclear weapons until after Stalin's death in 1953 although they had exploded their first atomic bomb in 1949—much earlier than our underestimates of their technological capability had indicated. Stalin, a typical revolutionary of the old school, preferred to cling to the traditional Russian concept of surface warfare, primarily relying on massive artillery, and thereby delayed effective recognition of the far-reaching implications of nuclear weapons.

After his death, however, Russian military experts finally convinced the Soviet rulers that the combination of nuclear weapons and long-range delivery systems made a successful surprise attack on the United States mainland entirely feasible. The attractiveness of such an attack was undoubtedly enhanced very much by the exciting prospect of neutralizing the Strategic Air Command whose long-range bombers represented the most potent deterrent to Communist aggression in the Free World. Once the Soviets adopted the concept of the nuclear surprise attack, they greatly accelerated the development of strategic weapons, with growing emphasis on ballistic missiles and space vehicles.

The tremendous expansion of the Soviet's military power can serve but one purpose—aggression. Historically, dictators and rulers who created a large and expensive military establishment were compelled to use it at one time or another in order to justify the sacrifices exacted from their subjects for creating and maintaining such an establishment. Innumerable precedents along this line make it appear highly improbable that the Soviet rulers can continue indefinitely to strengthen the offensive power of their gigantic military machine without applying it to some profitable objective.

Their insistent claims that the sole purpose of the military buildup is to protect Russia against American aggression are disproven compellingly by the record. If it had been our intention to attack the Soviet Union, we would have done so when our military superiority was still so overwhelming that we could have destroyed Russia with impunity. The free nations of the world are well aware of our peaceful intentions toward Russia. They gave this conviction vivid expression in the spring of 1958 when they refuted, in the strongest terms, the Soviets' complaint in the United Nations Security Council that training flights of the Strategic Air Command's bombers constituted a "threat" to them.

The fact that our national policy dictates a purely defensive military strategy has been proved time and again, even where it meant serious harm to the cause of democracy. When the Hungarian people rose against their Communist oppressors in the expectation that we would come to their aid, we shrank from the threat of military intervention although the Soviets, at that time, would have had no choice but to fold their tents and quietly move out of Hungary. We sacrificed the lives of over 50,000 Americans in Korea because we did not wish to use nuclear weapons against Red China although we could have ended and won that war virtually overnight. We permitted Castro to build up a Communist stronghold at our doorstep although we could have eradicated this festering cancer in our hemisphere without risk and without working up a sweat. These and many other examples should convince even our enemies that we are exercising the utmost restraint and intend to use our tremendous military power only for defending ourselves and our allies.

In contrast, the aggressive character of the Soviet military effort is demonstrated in many ways. Soviet military doctrine and organization as well as the structure of the armed forces are designed primarily for offense. But while articles and statements by Soviet leaders and military experts have provided a fair amount of information on the constitution and employment of their armed forces, few data have been released concerning actual numbers and deployment. The Soviets have been particularly secretive about their missile effort, but there can be no doubt that they possess sizable numbers of ballistic missiles, of both intercontinental and intermediate range, with good accuracy and reliability.

Because of their unique characteristics, ballistic missiles offer great advantages to an aggressor who plans to destroy his intended victim's retaliatory forces through a surprise attack. The Soviets are well aware of these advantages, and it would be folly to assume that they may hesitate or be unable to exploit them to the fullest, for they have both the technical and industrial capability of producing missiles in almost any desired quantities. Moreover, they have something that we lack—a system which permits them to cloak their missile effort in the utmost secrecy. Therefore, our knowledge of that effort cannot possibly match the information we have given the Soviets so freely with respect to our own missile development, production and deployment.

However, it is generally agreed that the Soviets have all of Western Europe zeroed in with IRBMs—Intermediate Range Ballistic Missiles—and that they possess sufficient numbers of ICBMs—Intercontinental Ballistic Missiles—to pose a grave threat to the United States. This direct threat will continue to mount in the days ahead, not only because of the rapidly growing stockpile of missiles in the Soviet arsenal, but perhaps even more so because of their advances in a related field—space. Here again our intense desire to look peaceful to the rest of the world makes us shrink from taking the steps necessary to meet any future Soviet threat from and in space.

In evaluating the military strength of the Soviets, it is frequently overlooked that their armaments serve not merely to permit a direct attack on the United States if, in the opinion of the Soviet hierarchy, such an attack should become necessary and feasible. In addition to providing their satellites with technical help and machinery for producing armaments, they have also given vast quantities of arms, directly or indirectly, to "neutral" nations which in one way or another were duped into serving the Communist cause. In doing so, the Soviets have managed either to start or fuel brushfire conflicts throughout the world, in the expectation of thus throwing us off balance and forcing us to spread our own military resources too thin.

But the military aspects of the Communist threat represent just one phase of the most insidious and gigantic plot in history. There are the economic, technological, political, ideological and other phases, all designed for one objective only, and that is the accomplishment of the ultimate Communist goal of total world domination. What is worse, some of our own people, ranging from subversives to supposedly intelligent and patriotic citizens, seem anxious to have us destroy ourselves, thus making the job that much easier for the Soviets.

These, then, are some of the factors that underscore the gravity of the Communist threat. This threat continues to grow, not only because our citizens often fail to appreciate its scope and nature, but also because the Soviets are determined to keep widening the gap between our weaknesses and their strengths. Uninhibited by any concern for the rights and dignity of human beings, they can further their goals by making effective use of the powers inherent in a firmly entrenched dictatorship.

We can meet the Communist threat only by making equally effective use of the even greater powers inherent in a democracy and free economy. This is quite a challenge because we must match the ruthless effectiveness of a dictatorship without matching its methods. I am confident that this can be done, but we must find a way of doing it without destroying politically and economically what we are trying to protect militarily.

Communism, as we know it today, is international in scope but national in character. It was bred by Russians and reared on Russian soil. Soviet Communism was built on the shoulders of the Russian masses. The unprecedented power of the Soviet hierarchy—the small group of actual rulers—is, in effect, the sum total of all the small fragments of individual power which the Russian people handed over to what they thought were their liberators and benefactors.

If, at any time in the future, the Russian masses should succeed in wresting these powers from the dictators and returning them to their rightful owners, the people, Soviet Communism would collapse because it has no other foundation. This, in turn, would greatly weaken if not destroy Communism in those countries to which it had been "exported" by the Soviets, provided these countries have not, in the meantime, modified the Soviet import so as to suit their own national characteristics. Communist China is the prime example.

Because of these factors, the character and mentality of the Russian people are of vital interest to us. They provide important clues in trying to learn something more conclusive about the implications, duration and also the weaknesses of the Communist threat even though the people themselves do not contribute directly to that threat.

On a whole, the Russian is more interested in problems that concern him or his family than in those that concern foreigners hundreds or thousands of kilometers away. He has many good reasons for being wary of war, and no reason whatever for wanting war with the United States or anyone else. The housewife in Moscow, the farmer in the Ukraine and the machinist in Leningrad have as much to lose and as little to gain from a war as the housewife in New York, the farmer in Iowa and the machinist in Detroit.

This does not mean that the average Russian is pro-American. He is neither pro-American nor anti-American; he is strictly pro-Russian. Few of these people ever had any personal contacts with Americans, and what limited knowledge they have about America, they have gained primarily from the rigidly controlled public media. For obvious reasons, they get all the news about the United States that is unfavorable and little, if anything, that is favorable. Conversely, great care is taken to play up news items which make the Soviet leadership appear in a favorable light and vice versa.

As a result, most Russians have no reason to suspect that the American way of life is any better than theirs. They have a vague idea of our country's wealth and industrial might. But they have been led to believe that this entails no advantages for common people like themselves, but benefits only the "capitalist exploiters." Even if they have an inkling of the higher standard of living in the United States, they do not compare their own standard to something they know so little about but to something the older ones among them still remember—the worse standard of living and life in Czarist Russia.

The Russians are a well-disciplined people and always have been. Every facet of their daily lives is regulated by some law or directive. There is little need for prodding them into obedience because generations of tyrannical rule have bred into them a wholesome respect for the law and the forces behind the law. As human beings, they undoubtedly like to grumble occasionally about the weight of their chains. But they know from experience that venting one's anger can be a costly pastime. I should imagine that no Russian ever complained to the Soviet Air Force about being bothered by sonic booms or demanded the closing-down of a missile site near his town.

It is difficult for us to conceive how and why human beings tolerate life in the police state that is the Soviet Union. But it must be remembered that such a life is not new to the Russians. It is a heritage which is accepted as a not-too-desirable but inescapable part of their traditional way of life. In fact, dictatorship itself is not a novelty on the Russian scene because there are many striking parallels between Soviet dictatorship and Czarist tyranny.

Even if, at some time in the future, the iron rule over the minds and bodies of the Russian people should be relaxed— which appears quite improbable at the moment—it is rather doubtful that propaganda from abroad, no matter how skillful, could cause serious disaffection among the masses toward the Communist regime or even spark uprisings similar to those that eventually led to the overthrow of the Czarist rule.

The present regime has been in power since 1917, which

means not only that it is firmly entrenched but also that most Russians have never known any other kind of government. Indications are that the majority of the people has been sold effectively on the merits of their regime and, in fact, believes that it will ultimately supplant all other forms of government throughout the world.

The Soviet propaganda machine has been exceedingly effective in convincing the masses that much, if not most, of the recent scientific progress is of Russian origin. The generous plaudits of the whole world following the first Sputnik launching and subsequent space achievements served further to strengthen the popular conviction that Russian technology has outstripped that of most or perhaps all other nations, including the "capitalist" United States.

Another important achievement of the Communist regime, as far as the Russian people are concerned, are the spectacular improvements in the field of education. Illiteracy, which was appallingly high under the Czarist regime, has been reduced rapidly through compulsory education. Advanced education is now available to all, not only to the children of wealthy families and the nobility as had been the case before. This means a great deal to the Russians because, predominantly European in character, they show much respect for the privileges ensuing from education and, therefore, hold great esteem for the educated.

I have little doubt that, to the average Russian, it is immaterial whether or not the Soviets have ulterior motives in fostering education among the masses. If, for instance, propaganda from abroad were to tell him that the principal purpose of the Communist educational program is to achieve military supremacy through technological superiority, he would probably fail to see anything wrong with that, quite to the contrary. But he would heatedly deny any claim that the ultimate objective of Russia's military buildup is to permit successful aggression against the United States.

One important reason for the relative ineffectiveness of propaganda from abroad is the fact that, traditionally, Russians are suspicious of foreigners, and for good reasons. Fourteen times since 1800, hostile troops have crossed Russia's western border. It has been attacked by Mongols, Tartars, Poles, Swedes, Frenchmen and Germans, all of whom left indescribable devastation in their wake.

In 1812, the Russians had to set the torch to Moscow to turn Napoleon's ambitious invasion into a disastrous rout. In what the Russians call the "Great Patriotic War," World War II, the city of Stalingrad in effect repeated the sacrifice of Moscow in turning back the ferocious legions of a would-be Napoleon— Adolph Hitler. But before the last Nazi stormtrooper had been driven from Russian soil, terrible destruction had been wrought and, according to conservative estimates, some twenty million Russians had lost their lives, about 10 percent of the total population.

It is, therefore, not surprising that the Russian people are tired of wars and wary of foreigners who, time and again, have forced these costly wars upon them. But the Russians are also a very patriotic people and, regardless of their personal feelings and convictions, would not hesitate to again give their all in the defense of their homeland if it were once more threatened by foreign enemies.

And that is exactly what the wily propaganda machine of their rulers keeps pounding into them. They are made to believe that the capitalist system entails a constant succession of periods of artificial prosperity and genuine depression of ever increasing magnitude, and that the capitalists have no other way of turning depression into prosperity than through war. The next major depression in the United States, the Russians are told, will practically force the "American imperialists" to start a war against Russia—its most formidable competitor— which must, therefore, be prepared to defend itself.

With this and similar shrewd appeals to their patriotism, the Russian people are systematically being conditioned for the inevitability of war and made to accept the oppressive buildup of the Soviets' vast military establishment, not as preparation for

Soviet aggression, but as a necessary expedient for deterring and repelling foreign aggression.

It has often been suggested in this country that the Soviets were creating a "Frankenstein" with their immense educational program. In other words, as the Russian people become better educated, they should be in a better position to recognize Communism for what it really is. And, as the number of enlightened Russians grows, their influence could be expected to increasingly weaken the foundations of the Soviet dictatorship until it would no longer be a threat to other nations.

But experience has shown that education is not necessarily an antidote to Communism. True, educated citizens from the Communist countries, especially those who have gained more than average knowledge of conditions in the West, continue to seek asylum in the democracies, leaving privileges and all behind. However, they constitute only a small percentage which, moreover, includes persons who have defected for reasons other than political ones.

On the other side of the ledger, there are large numbers of well-educated and, frequently, well-to-do people in the democracies, including our own, who overtly or covertly support the Communist cause even though they had every opportunity to compare the merits of the two systems on the basis of facts and personal knowledge.

It should, therefore, not surprise us that Russians with considerable education, intelligence and contacts with their colleagues in the West profess to be avowed Communists. Actually, many of the Russian intellectuals are not educated in our sense. Especially the new generation of professional people is knowledgeable mainly in one particular, narrow specialty and, hence, a more valuable asset to the Communist program, which has neither need nor sympathy for broadly educated individuals.

The importance of the Soviet intelligentsia is surpassed only by that of the Communist Party. The relative size of the Party, which reportedly has only some 11 million members representing 7.5 percent of the adult population, is not at all indicative of the tremendous power it wields over the country and over the 220-odd million Russians who are not Party members. To appreciate the scope and magnitude of this power, we must understand that the Communist Party is not a political party in our sense. It is rather an ingenious and complex tool designed to give a very few men at the top of the Party pyramid unchallenged and unlimited authority to pursue the objectives of the communist doctrine.

The Party permeates and controls every facet of life and activity in Russia, making certain that everybody and everything serve its purposes. Party members at all except the highest echelons make no major decisions but dutifully carry out the decisions of the bosses or ruthlessly see to it that they are being carried out, freely using the Secret Police, military forces, public media or any other tool at their command. Thus, the Party's well-oiled machine gives the Soviet rulers push-button control over the combined human and material resources of Russia and her satellites.

Rigidly disciplined, the Party members know only too well that, under the Communist system, failures must be attributed to the individual rather than to the system or ideology. They are resolved not to fail or let their subordinates fail because, as success is rewarded liberally, failure is punished severely which, in this kind of society, is a rather unpleasant prospect.

If the Soviet rulers should decide today or at any time in the foreseeable future to start World War III through an attack on the United States, they can count on these men, the stony-hearted members of the Communist Party, to carry out their orders—efficiently, promptly, and without asking any questions.

Who, then, are these rulers, men so omnipotent that one command from them could plunge the whole world into a nuclear war? The answer lies in the Soviet form of dictatorship.

There are, broadly speaking, two types of dictatorship—dictatorship of an individual and dictatorship of a system. The former is founded on the unique personality, inexplicable magnetism and limitless ambitions of an individual. When he passes out of the picture, for any one of a great number of reasons, there is usually no one of his stature to take his place. In the subsequent struggle among his former lieutenants, the dictatorship disintegrates and, as a rule, is replaced by a more liberal form of government. With certain qualifications, the rules of Nero, Napoleon, Mussolini and Hitler represent such transitory, one-man dictatorships.

Stalin's despotic absolutism led many people in this country to assume that his was another one-man dictatorship and that, upon his death, the Communist regime would suffer the usual fate of dictatorships founded solely upon the powers of an individual. But the Communist dictatorship is founded on the system, not the individual.

The Communist system makes it possible for a strong man to become a dictator but, no matter how strong he may be, the system that made him can also break him. When he dies or falls victim to the system, others are ready and waiting to take his place. There will be a bitter struggle for his job and, whoever emerges victorious in the end, will make what may seem sweeping changes in order to consolidate his position or reward those who have helped him. But regardless of what changes may have been made by him, nothing has changed as far as the system is concerned.

The precarious position of a dictator in the Soviet Union was strikingly illustrated by the fate of Nikita S. Khrushchev. As the First Secretary of the Communist Party and dominant member of the Presidium of the all-powerful Central Committee, and as Russia's Premier (Chairman of the Council of Ministers), he held powers which fairly matched those held by Stalin, his predecessor. Yet, in October 1964, the man believed to be the unchallenged master of the Soviet realm was booted out of office and power.

To reach the top in the "self-cleaning" Soviet political system, Khrushchev had to fight and virtually crush some very influential and popular opponents. When I met him during my visit to Russia, he impressed me as a very tough man, both physically and mentally. But the men behind him appeared to be equally tough. There could be little doubt that, some day,

Khrushchev would no longer be the top-man, for one reason or another, and that these men would battle for his place.

As these lines are being written, Leonid I. Brezhnev has assumed the leadership of the Communist Party as its First Secretary, and Aleksei N. Kosygin occupies Khrushchev's other job, that of Premier. But the struggle behind the scenes continues, and when the dust finally settles another dictator will emerge as Khrushchev's successor.

Whoever will win out, will again "liquidate" some potentially dangerous comrades and make some "jurisdictional" changes. Perhaps he will tear down the memory of Khrushchev as Khrushchev has torn down the memory of Stalin. But no matter who will succeed Khrushchev and when, there will be no change in the Communist objectives nor any relaxing in their pursuit. The "hierarchy" will see to that.

The Communist "hierarchy" begins, theoretically, with the All-Union Party Congress which, however, serves merely as a rubber stamp and a convenient forum for propaganda or policy pronouncements. The top leadership is represented by the Central Committee of the Party which, in turn, is headed by the 16-man Presidium, formerly known at the "Politburo." This Presidium and the Party's "Secretariat" represent the pinnacle of the Party pyramid, the heart and brain of the Communist conspiracy, the real Soviet hierarchy. Khrushchev could not stay in power for a minute once he had lost its support.

And there is the very root of the Communist threat. For the Soviet rulers are not like the leaders of other nations with whom one can reason and conclude agreements to be approved and honored by the people whom they represent. Despite their enormous power, they are themselves mere pawns of the Party and must abide by its inflexible rules. It is not their prerogative to decide whether to steer a more moderate and conciliatory course or whom to spare, except as a temporary expedient. Communism means total conquest and, therefore, permits of no compromise.

Pawns of the Party and pawns of the Communist system, the members of the glittering hierarchy are the Soviets' top men only because and as long as they carry out the Soviets' top job—directing the unwavering and uncompromising pursuit of the Communist objectives.

With the power which they derive from the strength of the Russian people and with the fantastic tools which the nuclear revolution has given them, the Soviet rulers are resolved to accomplish all that the Communist threat implies.

4. What Price Peace?

THE greatest challenge that faces the leaders of the Free World today is to prevent the Communist threat from exploding into a nuclear war and, at the same time, stem the tide of Communist expansion around the globe.

As pointed out earlier, the Soviet rulers themselves endeavor to achieve their objectives through means other than a major war, not because of compassion or compunction, but because such a policy entails far less risk and expense to them. Its efficacy has been demonstrated to their entire satisfaction by the huge gains it has brought them in the past. If similar gains could be made just as easily and "peacefully" in the future, the Soviets would have no reason to resort to nuclear aggression and would use it merely as a club to hold over the heads of such obstinate "nonconformists" as the United States.

Indeed, it seems that almost no one in this whole wide world of ours really wants war nor desires anything more earnestly than to live in peace and friendship with his neighbors. With everybody loving everybody else, it certainly should not be too difficult for representatives of the world's countries and peoples to get together and resolve, once and for all, the many major and seemingly minor issues that continue to flare up in local crises and armed conflicts.

If member nations of the United Nations, representing the majority of the world's population, are sincere in their desire for peace—and, apparently, all of them are or profess to be— they can be expected to be just as sincere in their efforts to eliminate, one by one, the existing obstacles to a lasting and secure peace.

Since its establishment in 1945, the United Nations has worked unceasingly and valiantly toward this objective. There have been gratifying successes and some disappointing failures. But the very concept of the United Nations should make it possible eventually to banish aggression and war from the international scene forever, provided its member nations exhibit intelligent and tolerant understanding of each other's peculiar problems, the determination to solve these problems to mutual satisfaction, and justifiable faith in the integrity of each other's governments in abiding by the agreements reached. Surely, qualities such as these are not too much to expect from civilized people!

But once before in our lifetime, the civilized people of the world have tried desperately—and unsuccessfully—to cope with the danger of a global war. Then as today, countries threatened by aggression were willing to pay almost any price for peace. Then as today, the democratic nations attempted to prevent aggression by resolving the explosive issues of the day at the conference table instead of on the battlefield.

On September 29, 1938, British Prime Minister Neville Chamberlain had flown to Germany for his memorable final meeting with the Nazi dictator Adolf Hitler in Munich. An agreement was reached, even though at a terrible price—the freedom and independence of Czechoslovakia. From the windows of the traditional Downing Street residence of England's prime ministers, Chamberlain showed a joint memorandum to the cheering crowd and exclaimed: "This is the second time there has come back from Germany to Downing Street peace with honor. I believe it is peace in our time."

This "peace in our time" lasted for exactly eleven months—

until the early dawn of September 1, 1939, when Hitler's legions invaded Poland and lit the fuse to World War II. Thus, the sacrifice of Czechoslovakia had bought the world, at best, eleven more months of uneasy peace. Moreover, it gave Hitler an exaggerated opinion of both his own strength and the weakness of his opponents. The Munich Agreement was ultimate proof to him that the democracies were afraid to fight and incapable of stopping him. Therefore, this agreement not only failed to prevent him from starting World War II; it actually encouraged him to start it.

Hitler's appraisal of the British proved to be wrong and his undoing. For that matter, Chamberlain's policy of appeasement by no means reflected the convictions of all his colleagues. As Winston Churchill reports in *The Gathering Storm,* the First Lord of the Admiralty, Duff Cooper, resigned in protest and attacked the Munich Agreement in a passionate address. His address was such an uncanny assessment of dealings with dictators that many parts of it can be applied to the current situation merely by changing names.

For instance, Cooper said:

"The Prime Minister [Chamberlain] has believed in addressing Herr Hitler through the language of sweet reasonableness. I have believed that he was more open to the language of the mailed fist. . . . The Prime Minister has confidence in the goodwill and in the word of Herr Hitler, although, when Herr Hitler broke the Treaty of Versailles, he undertook to keep the Treaty of Locarno, and when he broke the Treaty of Locarno, he undertook not to interfere further, or to have further territorial claims in Europe. . . . Still, the Prime Minister believes that he can rely upon the good faith of Hitler!"

There are many striking parallels between world conditions in the 1930s and conditions today. Again we must deal with the expansionist designs of a ruthless dictatorship, fully prepared and ready to attain its ends through another world war. Again, one sovereign nation after the other is forced or tricked into submission, with the rest of the world watching in impotent anger. Again people everywhere wonder what it will take to buy "peace in our time," a peace with honor.

With the specter of a nuclear holocaust haunting nations all over the globe, the desire for peace is even more intense and universal today than it was at the time of the Munich Meeting. As a result, there is considerable public agitation, especially in some of the Western democracies, for effecting compromises that would help to reduce, if not eliminate, the danger of another world war. It is, of course, realized that the issue is primarily between the United States and the Soviet Union. But there can be no doubt that the policies which these two countries will choose to pursue toward each other will profoundly affect the fate of their respective allies as well as that of most neutral or "uncommitted" nations. (The implications of Communist China's budding nuclear capability will be discussed in a subsequent chapter.)

It is, therefore, not surprising that a great many methods have been proposed and are being promoted actively, both in this country and abroad, for neutralizing or resolving the conflict between the Soviets and ourselves, and thereby to prevent a global war. The most widely discussed approaches for achieving these ends are the following:

1. NEGOTIATED PEACE. This approach entails nonaggression and friendship pacts or similar agreements, negotiated either through the facilities of the United Nations or at personal meetings of the heads of the nations concerned, such as "Summit Meetings."

The obvious question we must ask ourselves is whether there is any possibility at all of reaching an agreement with the Soviet Union that would effectively eliminate all threat of further Communist aggression of any type and in any form—military, political, economical. The answer must be in the negative so long as the Communist code of ethics brazenly declares as moral whatever furthers the Communist cause and as immoral whatever opposes that cause.

However perplexing this unique concept of morality may

seem to us, we must accept it as the standard of conduct governing all actions of the Soviets if we are to arrive at a realistic
appraisal of the value of their international commitments. For
here lies the explanation for the long and sordid history of treaties, agreements and nonaggression pacts which not only were
violated flagrantly by the Soviets but, in the cases of Latvia,
Lithuania, Estonia and others, served merely to permit subsequent conquest with little or no force.

A fully documented study of nearly one thousand Soviet treaties, published by the Senate Subcommittee on Internal Security, showed that the Soviet Union "had broken its word to
virtually every country to which it ever gave a signed promise."
Even in our dealings with the Soviets we have experienced
enough treachery to fill a book. Since 1943, when the Soviets
were supposedly our comrades-in-arms, they have violated most
of some 40 agreements involving specific promises.

From the Soviets' point of view, the sole purpose of an agreement is to provide them with a temporary advantage. If such an
agreement entails the slightest modification or change in the
established Communist objectives, the Soviets would consider it
"immoral" to abide by that agreement any longer than it serves
to enhance the achievement of these objectives.

Despite our knowledge of and experience with the Soviet
code of ethics in international relations, we have always been
willing to meet with the Soviets and even to enter into new
agreements with them. In relations between individuals, no
sane person would ever deal again with another person who has
broken his solemn word as frequently as the Soviets have
broken theirs. But political expediency often demands a more
tolerant attitude toward one's former, present or potential adversaries.

We must continue to show good faith and, regardless of all
setbacks, prove to the world and the Soviets that nothing can
change our desire to negotiate for a lasting peace under mutually acceptable conditions. It is, however, one thing to meet
and to make agreements with the Soviets, knowing full well
what to expect, and quite a different thing to accept any treaty

or pact with the Soviet Union as adequate protection for our nation's security. This would no longer be "political expediency"; this would be national suicide.

Lack of good faith on the part of the Soviet Union is by no means the only barrier to a negotiated peace. Even if we could negotiate with the Soviets in the firm conviction that they would abide by whatever agreements might be reached, there is little likelihood that a mutually acceptable compromise could be worked out. Both we and the Soviets want peace, but we want it for different reasons and on totally different terms.

Our ultimate terms are plain and straightforward because we want peace for peace's sake. We have no designs on the territory or sovereignty of other nations as we proved, for instance, when we granted the Philippines their promised independence. Too, we have much to lose and nothing to gain through a war; our victory in World War II cost us dearly and brought us no material gains whatever. Hence, we are asking nothing for ourselves. We are asking merely to ensure a lasting, all-out peace through an ironclad ban on international piracy, restoration of honesty and mutual faith among nations, and adherence to the golden rule in international relations.

But these unselfish terms are unacceptable to the Soviets because their ultimate terms cannot possibly fall short of their ultimate objectives. They do have designs on the territory and sovereignty of other nations as they have demonstrated frequently and convincingly. They, too, have much to lose through a war but also much to gain, in their estimation. Most of all, they could not accept and abide by our terms without renouncing the objectives of the Communist doctrine, which the self-perpetuating Communist system will never permit them to do.

For all these reasons, I am convinced that, for a long time to come, there is no hope for a negotiated peace which could serve as an acceptable safeguard against Communist aggression.

2. APPEASEMENT. This approach covers a broad range of policies designed to avert war at all cost, from actual submission to

Soviet mandate to a long series of ever greater concessions which, inevitably, would lead to submission also.

In *Modern Arms and Free Men,* Vannevar Bush, one of our foremost scientists, said: "We have heard much from the prophets of doom, and their cry is that the situation is so desperate that any alternative to war is preferable, or almost any alternative." These words were written in 1949, and even though the "prophets of doom" should have learned their lesson since, their cry is still being heard.

There is, for instance, the cry of another famous contemporary who proclaimed: "Rather Red than dead!" I am confident that the vast majority of the American people would passionately reject such ignominious defeatism and, instead, proclaim: "Rather dead than Red!" That is how the Hungarian men, women and even children felt who fought the Soviet tanks on their streets with their bare fists, only to be crushed to death or mowed down by machine guns. That is how thousands upon thousands of people throughout the ages have felt when they faced torture, starvation and hungry lions rather than bow to tyrants and renounce what they believed in.

Indeed, there is one sure way of surviving without inviting the horrors of a nuclear war, and that is to accept the fate of Poland, of Czechoslovakia, of the Soviets' other satellites. There are still cities left in these countries, and none of their citizens has been killed by hydrogen bombs. But let those of their citizens who escaped Communist bullets, bayonets and brutality tell the appeasers in this country and in the rest of the Free World what it means to be "Rather Red than dead!"

Of course, instead of giving the Soviets everything they ask for all at once, we could give it to them piecemeal, fighting at the conference table for every little concession. The utter folly of such a policy has been proven time and again, as it was proven in Munich when it served to precipitate rather than avert World War II.

Appeasement, by whatever name, is unworthy of a great nation such as ours because it means meek submission to blackmail despite the knowledge that a blackmailer will never cease his insatiable demands until he has taken everything from his victim.

3. COEXISTENCE. This policy is based on *limited* agreements and understandings with the Soviets which are considered to be to mutual advantage and are neither in violation of our principles nor require a modification of the Communist doctrine. We can expect the Soviets to abide by agreements intended to enhance the status of coexistence, so long as these agreements give them a free hand to pursue the Communist objectives by any means short of general war. Conversely, coexistence gives us supposedly a free hand in our continued efforts of combating Communism through diplomatic, economic and similar means.

With certain qualifications, this policy is in effect at present and has been in effect for some time. It permits a status of "negotiated stalemate" or "armed neutrality" which the Soviets prefer to call "coexistence." This rather euphemistic term helps to lend weight to their emphasis on the "peaceful battle of ideologies" and thus to hide their true intentions behind the cloak of international respectability.

But whatever their motives, there can be no doubt that the Soviets are decidedly in favor of coexistence, provided we are willing to play the game according to their rules. If they can achieve their objectives in the tolerant atmosphere of coexistence and save themselves a costly war in which they are directly involved, they would be that much ahead of the game.

The Soviets' favorable attitude toward coexistence is shared by a great many people in the Free World although, obviously, for different reasons. These reasons range from actual belief in the Soviets' professed peaceful intentions to the hope that, in the "peaceful battle of ideologies," the principles of democracy will, in the end, prevail over those of communism. Subconsciously, however, most people on our side who believe in the practicality of coexistence, *want* to believe in it because it represents a more promising way of averting war than meaningless peace pacts, and a more honorable way than appeasement.

The problem is that coexistence, cold war, "negotiated stalemate," "armed neutrality" or whatever it may be called by future historians, does not *prevent* Communist aggression but, at best, postpones it and, in effect, lays the groundwork for it. Once the Soviets have reached the point in the coexistence era where their cold-war techniques can bring them no further gain and their progress toward their ultimate objectives is halted, they must and will resort to military action.

There is no need to dwell on the Soviets' cold-war techniques—propaganda, subversion, inciting and supporting "brushfire" wars, fomenting revolutions, and many more. Nor is there any need to stress again the tremendous gains these tactics have brought the Soviets, and the cost and losses they have entailed for the Free World.

It should, therefore, be evident that coexistence is not at all what its name implies, what the Soviets want the world to believe, and what many of our citizens and friends would like to believe. To those who are guided by facts instead of wishful thinking, coexistence is merely a high-sounding and captivating code word for the merciless cold-war phase of Communist aggression. And for those who are guided by wishful thinking it may be well to remember two statements by Nikita Khrushchev which explain quite clearly what the Soviets think of the prospects of coexistence.

At a Polish Communist Party meeting in Warsaw, in 1955, the erstwhile Soviet strongman as quoted said blandly: "We must realize that we [the Communist world and the West] cannot coexist eternally, for a long time. One of us must go to the grave. We do not want to go to the grave. They do not want to go to their grave either. So what can be done? We must push them to their grave."

Khrushchev reiterated his desire to act as the West's mortician at a Kremlin reception in November 1956 when he reportedly said: "If you don't like us, don't accept our invitations, and don't invite us to come to see you. Whether you like it or not, history is on our side. We will bury you!" Speaking to the National Press Club in Washington some two years later, Khrushchev explained that his oft quoted phrase

"We will bury you" did not mean he wanted to bury every American in the physical sense. What he meant was that capitalism was historically doomed and that communism would prevail.

So much for the "promise" of coexistence.

4. DISARMAMENT. Reduction of arms by mutual consent is, in many respects, part and parcel of the coexistence philosophy. The Free World's proponents of disarmament usually maintain that, if the democratic and communist ideologies can peacefully coexist side by side, there is little danger of war. If there is little danger of war, there is little need for big armaments. If there are no big armaments, there will be still less danger of war.

Such logic has a great deal of appeal to a world that not only longs for peace but also is tired of footing the ever-mounting bills for arms of increasing cost and drain on human and material resources. But this logic will not stand up under the weight of the facts. In the first place, the feasibility of an international agreement for disarmament is contingent upon the good faith of all parties concerned. Enough has been said about the value of agreements with the Soviets to make it clear that this factor alone would prevent us from accepting a disarmament pact as sufficient and sole protection against Communist aggression.

It could be argued that any agreement for disarmament would include stipulations for some method of "policing" its enforcement. But, so far, the Soviets have rejected every proposal that would entail unrestricted on-the-spot inspection as we have offered to accept. Moreover, the utter secrecy with which the Soviets have always surrounded their military effort and the ominous reasons for such secrecy make it highly unlikely that they will ever accede to any agreement that would require free access to their military installations and facilities. And even if the Soviets should have a sudden change of heart, the tremendous land areas under their control—much of it practically inaccessible—and the compactness of modern weapons, such as missiles with nuclear warheads, would make even the most elaborate inspection method ineffective unless it were backed by good faith.

I am reminded of the time after World War I when the victorious allies unsuccessfully sought to enforce the stipulations of the Versailles Treaty which were to prevent Germany from rearming. The story is told of the German laborer in a former munitions plant which had been converted to the manufacture of baby buggies. As his wife was expecting a child, he proceeded to smuggle out part after part, one each day, until he thought he had everything he needed to put together a baby buggy in his basement. When his wife asked him how he was coming along, he scratched his head. "I don't understand what is wrong," he said. "No matter how I put those darn parts together, all I get is a machine gun."

Agreements for the voluntary reduction of arms have been tried before and, invariably, have failed because, as long as there is a single nation that violates—or is suspected of violating—the terms of the agreement, no other nation can afford to lay down its arms. Moreover, in this day and age even the most elaborate international disarmament pact is meaningless from the start unless it is joined in good faith—and I emphasize *good* faith—by every nation on earth that possesses or is likely to possess nuclear weapons and the weapon systems to deliver them.

For instance, if the United States and Soviet Russia as well as their respective allies should ever reach the point where they could enter into a feasible disarmament agreement, it is highly improbable that Red China, intransigent and bent on aggression, could be induced to follow suit. How then could the United States and, for that matter, Soviet Russia afford to divest themselves of the very weapons they may need some day to defend themselves against vast hordes of nuclear-equipped Red Chinese?

By its very nature, a disarmament pact puts the potential defender, that is, the nation or nations which the pact is designed to protect, at a grave disadvantage. Complying scrupulously with the terms of the pact, he greatly weakens his defensive capability. The potential aggressor, on the other hand, can resort to a token reduction to evade suspicion or fool "inspectors" and, thereby, succeeds in retaining most of his original offensive capability. As a result, his margin of military superiority is increased and, contrary to the intent of the disarmament pact, aggression is enhanced.

I understand that this is exactly what happened as early as some 2,500 years ago. According to Dr. Hu Shih, eminent Nationalist Chinese scholar, two warring states in China concluded a disarmament pact in 545 B.C. in order to stop the fighting between them. One side was honest and disarmed, but the other state cheated and thus managed to gain military superiority without any effort on its part. The rest is history.

Since then, the annals of history record case after case in which attempts at voluntary disarmament not only have proved utter failures but actually caused wars rather than prevented them. Striking examples in more recent times are the post-World War I treaties for the reduction of arms and "renunciation of war" (Kellogg-Briand Treaty) which were disregarded or unilaterally scrapped by Hitler and thus helped set the stage for World War II. Hitler's audacious rearmament effort also points up another weakness of the disarmament principle, namely, the impossibility to enforce it against the will of one or more of the parties concerned.

Let us assume again that the United States and Soviet Russia have signed a disarmament agreement calling for an elaborate inspection system such as considered an "adequate safeguard" by our disarmament advocates. Let us further assume that a team of international inspectors has accidentally discovered a vast underground installation hidden somewhere in the Siberian wasteland where large quantities of missiles are being mass-produced or some revolutionary space weapon is being developed. What could we do about it? Dispatch formal protests? Tell the Soviets they are bad boys and, please, stop violating the agreement? The only thing we could do would be to try to rebuild our dismantled armament industry as rapidly as possible, knowing full well that we could never catch up with the Soviets again.

There just is no logic in disarmament as a means for doing away with war, just as there is no logic in disbanding our local police departments as a means for doing away with crime. Despite the protection of thousands of law enforcement agencies, some four serious crimes are committed in this country every single minute. I shudder to think what would happen in our cities and towns if we would dissolve all law enforcement agencies and dismiss all policemen. A ridiculous thought? No more ridiculous than to believe that we can live in this world without armed protection against international gangsters, robbers and murderers. Man simply has not yet reached the plateau where he can live with his neighbor without the mutual protection of *enforceable* laws. This is as true in our hometowns as it is on the international scene.

Despite all these facts and considerations our government has proposed a "Treaty on General and Complete Disarmament in a Peaceful World." It is difficult for me to decide whether the people who have drafted or are supporting this proposal actually believe that such a fantastic and unrealistic plan should be pursued or whether they are promoting it merely for the sake of propaganda, in the conviction that the Soviets will never accept it anyway.

But whatever the reasoning and motives behind the proposal for eventual complete disarmament, its implications are so ominous and far-reaching that I shall discuss them in some detail in the following chapter. The point I want to make here is that the age-old illusion of disarmament as a means for insuring eternal peace is still or again being actively supported by many of our citizens in responsible positions, in spite of the shocking lessons of history and the threat to our national survival.

Our nation's current drive toward disarmament is by no means confined to theoretical proposals and talk at the conference tables in Geneva and at the United Nations. Persuaded that the Soviets have suddenly turned peaceable and can be trusted after all, our government has actually started to go down the disarmament road, gravely impairing our future capability to defend ourselves against wanton aggression. Our military plans and programs for the years ahead appear to be designed to "slow the expensive arms race" in the innocent belief that the Soviets are doing likewise. And accepting Soviet assurances that their intentions in space are entirely honorable, the United States has blithely joined in a United Nations resolution banning the use of weapons in space, thus virtually conceding this promising medium to Soviet trickery. Ironically, just a few months before this resolution was accepted, in February 1963, the Commander in Chief of the Soviet Strategic Rocket Forces, Marshal S. S. Biryuzov, boasted in a radio interview that the Soviets can launch rockets from satellites at a command from earth.

Perhaps still more serious in its potential consequences is the "Treaty for a Partial Nuclear Test Ban" concluded between the United States, Great Britain and the Soviet Union in July 1963, and subsequently joined by scores of other nations, with the notable exception of France and Red China—the only other countries with an early nuclear strike potential. I stated my unequivocal opposition to the ratification of this treaty when I was called before the Congress in my capacity as both the Commander in Chief of the Strategic Air Command and Director of the Joint Strategic Target Planning Staff; that is, as the man most directly concerned with the military consequences of the test ban treaty.

I had arrived at my stand after very thorough soul-searching and extensive study of all the military and technical aspects involved. I realized that other high-ranking officers, who had also been asked for their opinion, had given the treaty half-hearted approval, perhaps in deference to their civilian superiors or because they believed that the political advantages might outweigh the military disadvantages. However, I felt that I had been called before the Congress as a military man and that, for this reason, it was my duty to express my honest and considered opinion, regardless of any other considerations. And that opinion was, and still is, that ratification of the treaty was *not* in the best interests of the United States.

An unclassified version of my testimony, which was given in executive session, was made available to the press and later published. Therefore, there is no need to discuss it here in detail. Summarizing briefly, I opposed the test ban treaty primarily for the following reasons: The Soviets had developed and detonated nuclear weapons of far higher yield than we had, and while the treaty, which still permitted underground testing, gave them the chance to catch up with our lead in small-yield nuclear weapons, it retarded our efforts to catch up with their lead in the high-yield area. Moreover, there is reason to believe that detonation of high-yield weapons may have certain effects which could seriously impair the operability and performance of our strategic missiles. Only testing in the atmosphere can determine the nature and gravity of these effects and permit the development of measures to counteract them.

Related to this problem is the incredible fact that we have never tested an Intercontinental Ballistic Missile all the way from launch to detonation of the warhead, despite my insistent urging to do so. Although our current military strategy places increasing emphasis on missiles, the test ban treaty now deprives us of every possibility to ascertain whether our ICBMs will really function as expected. I submit that this is the first time in our history that much or even most of the nation's striking power is to be entrusted to weapons that have never been fully tested operationally.

Incidentally, the claims that such and related testing would dangerously contaminate the atmosphere appear grossly exaggerated, according to the opinion of many highly qualified experts. The increase in the always present background radiation would be so slight as to be negligible and would indeed be an acceptable price for an indispensable contribution to the nation's security.

Another reason for my opposition to the test ban is best expressed in the following quotation:

We must test in the atmosphere to permit the development of those more advanced concepts and more effective, efficient weapons which, in the light of Soviet tests, are deemed essential to our security. Nuclear weapon technology is still a constantly changing field. If our weapons are to be more secure, more flexible in their use and more selective in their impact—if we are to be alert to new break-throughs, to experiment with new designs—if we are to maintain our scientific momentum and leadership—then our weapons progress must not be limited to theory or to the confines of laboratories and caves.

The above statement was not made by a "warmongering general" but by none other than the late President Kennedy. He made this significant statement in March 1962 when he announced resumption of nuclear testing after the Soviets had seen fit to break the then existing moratorium.

When my Congressional testimony was published, I received many hundreds of letters—a surprisingly high percentage from women—virtually all of which supported my stand enthusiastically. The most striking thing about these letters was the fact that the writers expressed grave concern not only about the test ban treaty but, even more so, about the trend it represented—the trend toward heedless disarmament. I am aware that the majority of our citizens, as indicated by the majority vote in the Senate, approved of the treaty. But I doubt that many of these citizens would have approved had they known all the facts, especially those that for reasons of security could not be discussed publicly. And I am confident that most of those citizens who did approve would not want to consider that treaty as the first and irrevocable step toward complete disarmament.

As a military man, I may be accused of lumping everything under the heading of disarmament that may tend to slow the arms race. In fact, the advocates of disarmament may call me narrow-minded and prejudiced because of my long and intimate association with that arms race. But I am no longer looking at the overall problem as a military man; I am looking at it as an American citizen who still is deeply concerned about the survival of this nation. I agree that disarmament is a noble goal —as is a world in which there is no longer need for policemen. I also agree that we should continue to explore the possibilities of slowing the arms race. But so long as our security demands that we stay in that race, I recommend that we had better make very certain that we are the ones who stay ahead, as we have managed to do to this day.

5. PREVENTIVE WAR. The most drastic measure this nation could take to forestall Communist aggression presumably is to attack the Soviets before they can attack us, that is, to launch what is popularly known as a "preventive war."

Some of our citizens advocate such a measure in the conviction that, whatever toll in lives and damage to our cities it might entail, it would be far less severe than the losses we could expect to suffer in a Soviet surprise attack which they believe is bound to come. Most other people in this country, however, are strongly opposed to the very idea that we would ever start any kind of war, not only because of moral reasons but also because of our traditional national policy against aggression. Actually, the concept of "preventive war" is too complex to justify conclusive opinions either for or against it.

Being highly controversial, this subject is usually avoided in public discussions. Perhaps there is too much concern that any reference to it might be interpreted as harmful "saber-rattling." Or perhaps it is felt that preventive war is too delicate a subject to be aired before the public.

But we should remember that there was also a time when public discussion on cancer, sex and mental illness was frowned upon, seriously impeding the promotion of better understanding of the problems involved. By the same token, I consider it important for the American people to understand the implications of preventive war and, through frank and open discussion, correct the many misconceptions that exist.

The term "preventive war" is, in itself, contradictory and rather misleading as it implies that war is to be prevented by starting it. Nor is it correct to assume that we can prevent the

Soviets from striking at us merely by striking first. Moreover, we may find it necessary to thwart Soviet actions other than outright aggression against this country.

As a rule, the term "preventive war" is applied indiscriminately to several different types of military operations which, generally, fall into one of three categories, best described as "pre-emptive war," "pre-emptive strike" and "assumption of initiative."

We speak of *pre-emptive war* if a nation has certain knowledge of an imminent attack by another nation and decides to deprive that nation of the advantage of the initiative by striking at it first. It is conceivable that we may be placed in that position with respect to Russia.

The decision to launch a pre-emptive war against the Soviet Union would be a very difficult one for the Congress or the President to make, even if our intelligence should have ascertained, beyond any doubt, that the Soviets were preparing to attack us within the next few days or hours. Regardless of how successful our initial attack might be, it could not possibly destroy the entire offensive capability of the Soviets. Some of their bombers and missiles would escape destruction and succeed in mounting a counterattack, exacting a high price with their nuclear payloads. But if there were no other way left to escape an imminent surprise attack, our government might well have to resort to a pre-emptive war which, even though it could not save us from heavy damage, would serve to keep our losses to a minimum.

In such a case, pre-emptive war would be considered the lesser of two evils because, by definition, it is the only alternative to enemy aggression. If we could have foreseen the Japanese attack on Pearl Harbor and been certain that Japan was determined to go through with its plans for aggression, a pre-emptive war against Japan not only would have been justified but also could have reduced our subsequent losses greatly and, probably, shortened the war considerably.

Nevertheless, there is relatively little likelihood of a pre-emptive war against the Soviet Union because, so long as there is the slightest hope that we can prevent a Soviet attack through diplomatic means or a strong posture of deterrence, our government, backed by the majority of the American people, would in my opinion be opposed to more drastic measures.

It could be argued that we have had ample strategic warning of the Soviets' intentions and may, therefore, expect that they will attack us if and when they feel confident that they can do so successfully and with relative impunity. It is, however, still within our power to keep their confidence from reaching that plateau and to continue discouraging Soviet aggression by means other than war.

Still, we cannot rule out the possibility that, despite all efforts to the contrary, the Soviets suddenly may decide to attack. If we should receive tactical warning of their attack shortly before or as it was being launched, our government probably would take immediate action designed to blunt the enemy's thrust. This is termed a *pre-emptive strike.* It differs from a pre-emptive war in that it occurs too late to prevent the enemy from mounting his attack but serves mainly to reduce its effectiveness. Nor would a pre-emptive strike, of necessity, entail a full-scale attack on the enemy's homeland, the use of nuclear weapons or, for that matter, lead to general war.

Referring again to the Pearl Harbor attack, let us assume that we had received tactical warning of the Japanese attack as their carriers were casting off. Obviously, we would have made every effort to intercept and destroy these carriers at the greatest possible distance from United States territory and thus prevent their aircraft from reaching it. This would have been a pre-emptive strike in which we would have taken the initial action. In retrospect, it is not at all certain whether that action would have resulted in all-out war with Japan because its military leaders had counted on the Pearl Harbor attack to deal American offensive strength in the Pacific a fatal blow.

Similarly, we might get tactical warning of a Communist attack on one of our or of our allies' military units, installations or territories, compelling us to take all actions necessary to prevent the enemy from accomplishing his objective. A pre-emptive strike under these conditions could well serve to deter general war rather than precipitate it because the enemy would have to assume that we would not risk all-out war unless we were fully prepared for it.

A third type of military action which is frequently referred to as "preventive war" is *assumption of the initiative*. A nation is said to assume the initiative if it undertakes military action, not because it is threatened by imminent aggression, but in order to achieve a major national objective or protect its national interests. For instance, the Japanese assumed the initiative in starting the war with the United States in 1941 because their leaders at the time had decided that this was the most expeditious way of attaining Japan's national objectives. If, at any time in the future, the Soviets should reach the conclusion that aggression against this country would be the most desirable and effective method of achieving their goals, they, too, would be assuming the initiative.

Conversely, we would be the ones to assume the initiative if we were to launch a surprise attack on Russia, not to prevent inevitable Communist aggression (which would be a pre-emptive war), but to protect our national interests. While it is very unlikely that we will ever go that far, we may have to assume the initiative in certain local situations. A case in point is the dispatch of American troops to Lebanon in 1958, which helped to resolve that particular crisis and, although it brought us no tangible gains, accomplished its purpose of safeguarding our interests in the Middle East.

We could afford to assume the initiative in this local conflict because the operation was conducted under an umbrella of military strength—backed by an unprecedented number of SAC bombers ready to strike at a moment's notice—which would have been adequate even if the crisis had developed into a full-scale war. This did not happen because of the very fact that we demonstrated our readiness for this contingency.

It is, therefore, evident that we may have to take military actions of various types which, with certain qualifications, might fall under the public's broad concept of "preventive war." Needless to say, such actions could never be undertaken by our military commanders unless decided upon and ordered by the civil authorities. However, so long as the possibility exists that we may have to resort to pre-emptive or initiative operations, military commanders in the field must be prepared to execute them instantly. For this reason, we must maintain adequate and combat-ready forces-in-being which are capable of immediate response in dealing with any foreseeable emergency.

Indeed, it would be a grave mistake to give the Soviets the impression that we would never strike first. The mere possibility that we may do so forces them to prepare themselves accordingly—including maintenance of an extensive warning system—which compounds their problems and detracts from their offensive strength.

But the most important reason why we must never commit ourselves irrevocably to a policy of not striking first is our obligation to our partners in mutual assistance pacts. As our government has made it clear that it will stand by its obligations under these agreements, it might be forced into the position of taking military action against the Soviet Union if that nation should attack one of our allies. Although such action might be undertaken without an attack on the United States proper, it could not be considered "pre-emptive" in the strictest sense of the word but would, in effect, be retaliatory. For an attack on any country in the Free World with which we have a mutual security agreement must be accepted as an attack on the United States itself. If we would ever give the Soviets—or Red China—the impression that we would never strike unless they attack United States territory, they would feel free to wage aggression against any other country in the Free World, without fear of reprisal on our part. At the same time, we would raise serious doubts in the minds of our allies that we intend to live up to our obligations to them when the chips are down.

There can be no doubt that pre-emptive military action of any type is not a desirable method for avoiding, averting or countering Communist aggression. But there are situations when it may prove necessary or less costly than any other action —or lack of action.

6. DETERRENCE. To discourage aggression of any type and scope through an overwhelming posture of military strength is, in my considered opinion, the most worthwhile and promising method of dealing with the Communist threat.

So long as a potential aggressor knows that, no matter how unexpected and massive his attack, he cannot prevent us from inflicting unacceptable damage upon him, he will be effectively deterred from undertaking such an attack. But deterrence is more than just weapons and men, and the threat to use them in retaliation to aggression. Deterrence is the sum total of many diverse elements which, in combination, serve to convince our enemies that if they choose to precipitate a nuclear war, the United States will survive and they will not.

When I referred to Duff Cooper's eloquent condemnation of the Munich Agreement, I spoke of his conviction that Hitler would not listen to the "language of sweet reasonableness" but only to the "language of the mailed fist." History proved Duff Cooper right. I am convinced that history will also prove right those of us who insist that the only language to which the Communists will listen is the language of deterrence, as symbolized by the emblem of the Strategic Air Command—the mailed fist.

5. The One-World Syndrome

I HAVE every reason to believe that the majority of the American people favors an unequivocal national policy of deterrence in preference to any of the other approaches for preserving peace. But I am not persuaded that many of these people know exactly what kind of peace they want and what ultimate objectives our policy of deterrence should be designed to achieve. I submit that there must be some agreement on these objectives before we can determine the means and ways of attaining them.

During my over seven years as Commander in Chief of the Strategic Air Command I talked to scores of diverse groups of leading citizens who visited SAC Headquarters because they had a deep and sincere interest in getting firsthand information on the Free World's most powerful military deterrent to aggression. Virtually all of these people—professional men and women, ministers, labor leaders, industrialists, businessmen— voiced their full support for maintaining a strong and credible military deterrent as the principal safeguard of an "honorable peace." But there was one question that came up quite frequently: For how long do we have to keep it up? The only answer my conscience permitted me to give was, "For as long as our survival is threatened; that is, indefinitely."

Occasionally the subsequent discussion would lead to another question, namely, whether the time would ever come when our survival might no longer be threatened and we could safely discard our weapons. This, in turn, would bring up the subject of one-world government as a means for ending the arms race, and I would find that quite a few of my listeners believed this to be a worthwhile goal, however difficult and distant it might be. But when I would question them regarding the implications and dangers of the one-world principle, it became patently clear that they had given little if any thought to it.

It is significant that these and many other people who firmly support a national policy of deterrence based on superior military strength are equally convinced or, at least hopeful, that one-world government offers the ultimate solution for the problem of survival in the nuclear age. Personally, I fail to understand how a person can profess to be willing to give his all for national survival and at the same time advocate a goal which, in effect, means surrender of our national sovereignty and integrity. Still, there is widespread belief in both the desirability and feasibility of one-world government and, indeed, much indication that we are going down that road. I call this the "one-world syndrome."

The dictionary defines "syndrome" as a "number of symptoms occurring together and characterizing a specific disease." I have been watching, with mounting concern, a variety of symptoms develop which characterize what I consider an emotional disease, namely, an almost pathological craving for escape from reality in trying to resolve the paradox of national survival through national suicide. That is why I speak of a "one-world syndrome."

I realize that those of us who insist on preserving what hundreds of thousands of Americans have fought and died for —a free and sovereign nation—may be called sentimental fools or reactionaries or unrealistic or warmongers by those who believe in the inevitability of one-world government. But discounting the invectives, pallid clichés and learned double-talk, the issue is clear: shall we continue indefinitely to preserve and protect our national integrity regardless of cost, or shall we work toward long-range survival by being willing to abandon nationhood in favor of one-world government?

Ours is still a democratic nation and it is, therefore, up to the American people to decide which road to survival they want to choose. The choice is by no means easy. The active proponents of one-world government have a very salable product to sell— peace without an arms race—and they are both vocal and convincing. Most of them are well-informed, intelligent and law-abiding citizens, many of them in prominent positions, who are just as sincere in their convictions as we, who disagree with them, are in ours. Unfortunately, however, our approach—survival through military supremacy—ostensibly entails far greater sacrifices and risks, and therefore has less appeal to those who seek a quick and easy way out. Still, it is the only approach which will permit *national* survival. This is the approach which we have followed to this day, and it has proved successful. The question before the American people now is whether we should continue to follow it throughout the indefinite future or whether we should march down the disarmament road toward the nebulous goal of one-world government.

The two approaches permit of no compromise because they point in exactly opposite directions. Therefore, in making their choice, our citizens must select the one or the other, realizing that once they have chosen the road to disarmament and one-world government, there can be no turning back. Too, the American people must be made to understand that whatever road to survival they may choose, they will have to pay a price for it, and here I believe lies the crux of the whole matter.

Obviously, survival means different things to different people, and the price they are willing to pay for it differs accordingly. Hence, any discussion of the price of survival has little merit unless there is agreement on the kind of survival we want to buy. The issue is not merely a matter of semantics or definition but one of attitude and, indeed, individual character.

Many people regard "survival" as something entirely physical, others as something economic or political or perhaps spiritual. But whatever his personal concept of survival, almost anyone will insist that it is all-inclusive and, in fact, representative of national survival. This does not mean that the term "national survival" by itself could serve the purposes of this discussion, because it represents too vague and intangible a thing to put a definite price tag on it.

There is also the question as to whether the exigencies of survival are viewed in the light of the cold war, hot war or both. Someone who has never seen real disaster obviously is less inclined to pay a high price for insurance against it than the person who has actually experienced it. In a broader sense, this human trait applies quite generally to the citizens of this country who, by tradition and experience, have come to take the safety of their tangible and intangible possessions for granted. Besides, the cold war seems too remote and has had too little direct impact on the life of the average American to arouse real concern over any acute threat that it may entail—except the threat of hot war.

Conversely, there has been so much irresponsible and unqualified talk of the utter futility of nuclear war as to convince many people that such a war simply cannot or must not happen. As a result, they have grown too complacent to prepare for it or so frightened that they are ready to pay any price for avoiding it.

It is, therefore, unrealistic to base our design for survival on the assumption that our citizens are agreed on the nature and scope of the threat which the nation faces in the years ahead, let alone on the steps to be taken to meet that threat. By the same token, we must recognize that the cost of meeting any threat to survival will be acceptable to the rank and file of our citizenry only under three conditions—it must ensure the kind of survival they desire; it must be within their means; and above all, it must be justifiable. In other words, people cannot be expected to make any sacrifices for meeting a threat unless they fully understand its implications.

Even as the concepts of survival vary, there are commensurate variations in the concepts of what constitutes an acceptable price for it, both as to magnitude and type. Generally speaking, the cost of survival falls into one or more of three areas, depending on the desires and character of the people concerned.

If the desire for purely physical survival is predominant, it may be bought by paying for it with non-physical values. This means, as a rule, that the threat of aggression can be averted by meeting the demands of the aggressor, even if it leads eventually to complete subjugation to his rule. Ironically, the price for this kind of peace entails not only the total loss of a people's sovereignty and supposedly inalienable rights but also a constant threat to their worldly possessions and lives—the very things they desired to protect.

Even if the concept of survival is extended to preservation of the nation's integrity, its price may include at least some curtailment of civic rights and liberties. Such curtailment, however, is voluntary and in conformance with democratic principles since it is entirely within the purview of the people or their elected representatives. It is they who decide as to when, for how long, in what manner and to what extent some of their civic rights should be curtailed in order to enhance the preservation of others. The important distinction is that they assign some rights to their elected government for as long as they deem necessary instead of ceding all their rights to a dictator, foreign ruler or supergovernment to exercise and hold at their discretion.

Nevertheless, it must be realized that "national survival," in its broadest sense, may require the temporary acceptance of certain restrictions or rules, including methods for their enforcement which may seem contrary to the tenets of democracy, especially in peacetime. Examples which we have experienced in the past include the institution of what amounts to compulsory military service, control of critical materials, rationing of scarce supplies, denial of passports for cause, some limitations in the right to strike essential industries and services, and a host of others.

The point is not whether these and related curtailments of civic rights and liberties are justifiable in a democracy but that a democracy cannot survive unless its citizens are willing to accept such curtailments as part of the price of survival. The grave danger here lies in the possibility that as the people continue to surrender more and more of their individual rights to their government, they may eventually have no longer the power or even desire to either halt the further deterioration of the democratic system or to restore it to its original status once the external threat to it has passed. This danger, too, is part of the price of survival.

A similar danger exists in the economic area. While ours is not actually a "controlled economy," it has been necessary to impose certain controls on private enterprise because of the far-reaching demands of our struggle for survival. However undesirable in a democracy, some degree of control is mandatory even in a free economy in order to prevent the mounting cost of survival from precipitating economic ruin. Again, there is the risk that control may lead to control until we reach the "point of no return" and have, in fact, a controlled economy.

This risk is growing more acute as we must find new ways of coping with the vicious spiral of ever higher defense expenditures—higher taxes—more inflation. Unfortunately, government controls can attack only the various *effects* of the spiraling cost of survival but not its underlying causes. This is due, primarily, to three reasons.

First, steady advances in military technology engender growing complexity and, in turn, greater cost. Second, the increasing requirement for advanced skills in the development, manufacture and operation of modern military equipment, compounded by the rising cost of labor at all skill levels, keeps inflating the price of survival. And, third, there is the huge expense for our foreign aid programs which are considered to be indispensable in enabling our allies, both economically and militarily, to help us contain the global spread of Communism.

In addition to the inherent political and economic dangers, the struggle for survival in the nuclear age entails the most ominous risk of all, namely, the risk of all-out nuclear war. Unless the American people are willing to accept that risk we cannot possibly survive as a nation and, for that matter, may actually invite such a war. It is, therefore, evident that our struggle for survival is not merely a matter of dollars and cents, and that the contribution of the average citizen to that struggle is not limited to paying taxes.

Indeed, the price of survival is as inclusive as the basic concept of "national survival," which is the unimpaired and perpetual preservation of the prime prerequisites of a true democracy—national security, political integrity, civil liberty, spiritual honesty, and physical safety.

The question arises whether these are the assets which the majority of our citizens wants to preserve, regardless of the cost and sacrifices and risks this may entail. I am confident that the answer is and will continue to be in the affirmative, as it has been in the past. Why is it, then, that so many of these very same citizens apply a different set of values to the proposition of one-world government as the ultimate means for ensuring survival?

The American people today are far more advanced, in many respects, than their forebears were only a generation ago. They have not only grown wealthier and stronger as a nation but, as individuals, are considerably more sophisticated, more knowledgeable and more interested with respect to national and international affairs. Nevertheless, there are many misconceptions and much apathy regarding the nature and scope of the threat to our survival.

Enjoying the highest standard of living of any nation in history, this country now finds itself in the role of both benefactor and protector of less fortunate nations and, at the same time, of the principal defender of democracy. Whether or not we aspired to this demanding role is beside the point. The fact remains that we have assumed the undisputed leadership of the Free World and, as a result, are the principal target for Communist aggression.

Our increasing involvement in international affairs has necessitated a radical revision in two of our traditional traits. For one, we learned that we could no longer afford the luxury of isolationism and had to extend, through a series of mutual security agreements, our area of national interests to most of the remaining free nations. Second, despite our innate dislike for all things military we had to create and now maintain the most powerful military establishment in the world.

This should not imply that Americans, by nature, are isolationist and pacifist. But in contrast to many Europeans, the average American had little reason to be concerned with the political problems and conflicts of other nations and, therefore, did neither desire nor expect to become involved in them. World Wars I and II demonstrated that Americans can and will fight for other countries once they are convinced that the security and welfare of their own country are at stake. But these wars also showed that the price of unpreparedness for defending our interests and those of our allies can be far higher than the price of sustained preparedness.

We failed to heed the lessons taught by World War I, primarily because the understandable desire to stay out of any further foreign wars, in which we had nothing to gain and much to lose, strengthened rather than lessened the forces of isolationism in this country. The attack on Pearl Harbor proved the futility of a purely defensive policy in a world which had become one vast battleground for global power politics. Again, we were poorly prepared to fight a war, and it took us years until we were in the position to take decisive action.

Fortunately, we had the human and material assets as well as the time to build up the most formidable war machine in military history. But there can be no doubt that if we should ever be subjected to a nuclear Pearl Harbor, we would have neither the time nor capability to augment the forces and weapons we might have in being at the time of the attack. In fact, we would have to fight and win the war with the forces and matériel that we would have left *after* a missile surprise attack.

It is obvious, therefore, that we must pay the price of survival in the face of the nuclear threat *before* that threat materializes instead of waiting until we are forced to react, as we could do and have done in meeting the lesser threats of the past. The

problem lies in getting the American people to appreciate the
singular nature and scope of the current threat to our survival
and thereby to gain their support in meeting a contingency that
may never arise—provided we are adequately prepared for it.

This seemingly paradoxical issue is not at all well understood
by the public. The impression persists that military preparedness is comparable to insurance against disaster, but this analogy overlooks the fact that insurance cannot prevent disaster; it
merely is designed to minimize its financial consequences. Conversely, military preparedness, as incumbent upon us today, has
two objectives—to prevent war under acceptable conditions
and, if it cannot be prevented, to win it so as to ensure our
national survival.

Because of the dramatic compression of time and the unprecedented devastation made possible by modern weapons, the cost
of pursuing these two military objectives is very high, but the
cost of failing to achieve them is prohibitive. These conclusions
may be axiomatic but they presuppose familiarity with certain
political and military factors which, in combination, represent
at once the least understood and the most serious threat to our
survival we have ever faced. I have found that many of our
citizens are either unfamiliar with these factors or confused by
the contradictory theories advanced by the avant-garde strategists. Therein, perhaps, lies much of the explanation why the
one-world proposition holds such curious attraction.

In contrast to the high price and grave risks involved in continuing our past and present policy of deterrence, the pursuit
of one-world government promises survival at little cost and no
risk. And in contrast to the wide disagreement in the deterrence camp as to what constitutes "adequate deterrence," the
proponents of one-world government profess to know exactly
what they want and how to achieve it.

The first step they advocate is to halt the international arms
race through various treaties and agreements, thus greatly reducing the cost of military preparedness and lessening the risk
of war. The next step is "general and complete disarmament,"
to be accomplished in three stages as proposed by the United

States Arms Control and Disarmament Agency in its "Blueprint for the Peace Race" which was submitted to the Geneva Disarmament Conference in April 1962. In the final stage of disarmament the "Parties to the Treaty would complete the reduction of their [military] force levels, disband systems of reserve forces, cause to be disbanded organizational arrangements comprising and supporting their national military establishment, and terminate the employment of civilian personnel associated with the foregoing." In addition, the Parties of the Treaty would "dismantle or convert to peaceful uses the military bases and facilities remaining at their disposal." The only forces and facilities they would be permitted to retain would be those agreed upon to be necessary for maintaining "internal order" and protecting "the personal security of citizens," that is, police forces.

The Foreword to this "Blueprint for the Peace Race," which has the enticing subtitle "Outline of Basic Provisions of a Treaty on General and Complete Disarmament in a Peaceful World," states: "An ultimate goal of the United States is a world which is free from the scourge of war and the dangers and burdens of armaments, in which the use of force has been subordinated to the rule of law, and in which international adjustments to a changing world are achieved peacefully." But as it is realized that there can be no "rule of law" and "peaceful international adjustments" without the use of some force, the Parties of the Treaty would contribute men and matériel to a United Nations Peace Force which would be progressively strengthened "until it had sufficient armed forces and armaments so that no state could challenge it."

On the surface, this Utopian scheme seems most attractive. The billions of dollars now being spent for maintaining huge national military establishments could be diverted to peaceful uses. The specter of nuclear war would fade away; brushfire wars would become unlikely and, should they happen, could be nipped in the bud by the all-powerful United Nations Peace Force. Uneasy coexistence and the "balance of terror" would yield to eternal friendship and cooperation among nations which thus would live happily ever after. And all of this could be bought virtually with the stroke of a pen. The price? Negligible in the estimation of the one-worlders—"merely" surrender of national sovereignty!

To be sure, the "Blueprint for the Peace Race" does not mention surrender of national sovereignty at all. However, it does say, "The Parties to the Treaty would undertake such additional steps and arrangements as were necessary to provide a basis for peaceful change in a disarmed world and to continue the just and peaceful settlement of all international disputes, whether legal or political in nature." This broad statement could apply to offshore fishing rights, airline fares, broadcasting frequencies and a host of other issues which are presently being discussed and settled on a nation-to-nation basis. Under the "Blueprint for the Peace Race" the International Disarmament Organization, through a "Control Council" and "Administrator," could unilaterally and arbitrarily assume settlement of any national and international issue which it considered to fall within its jurisdiction, thus making it in effect a one-world government.

And that is step three on the long road from "halting of the arms race" to the surrender of national sovereignty. Many supporters of one-world government shy away from defining their ultimate objective that bluntly. For instance, William C. Foster, Director of the United States Arms Control and Disarmament Agency which published the "Blueprint for the Peace Race," prefers to speak of "international machinery." He said, "But since deterrence or the balance of terror does not provide a satisfactory long-term solution, we must work toward the development of international machinery which gradually but ultimately can replace national military forces as guarantors of security."

Others are less circumspect in equating the cause of disarmament with that of one-world government. W. W. Rostow, who served among others as chairman of the Policy Planning Council of the Department of State, wrote:

. . . It is a legitimate American national objective to see removed from all nations—including the United States—the right to use substantial military force to pursue their own interests. Since this residual right is the root of national sovereignty and the basis for the existence of an international arena of power, it is, therefore, an American interest to see an end to nationhood as it has been historically defined.

Still more outspoken is the well-known educator Robert M. Hutchins, who served as Associate Director of the Ford Foundation and later became President of the Fund for the Republic. In a syndicated column in which he berates the Daughters of the American Revolution for advocating the teaching of American history in the schools, he avers: "No teacher could avoid pointing out that national sovereignty is synonymous with international anarchy. Disarmament and some form of world government are going to be necessary if the grandchildren of the DAR are going to survive."

These and innumerable other statements leave no doubt that the price we would have to pay for survival through disarmament and eventual world-government would be gradual surrender of our national sovereignty. This is a price which I consider far higher than the price we are paying for survival through deterrence and, in fact, a price which is utterly unacceptable to me and, I am sure, to the great majority of the American people. And what about the risks, as compared with the risks involved in our national policy of deterrence? Let us examine a few of them.

The gravest risk I see in the proposal for "general and complete disarmament" is the very existence of an all-powerful international police force which, according to the charter of the suggested International Disarmament Organization, no state, including the United States or any of its Western allies, would be able to "challenge." Presumably, there would be provisions to prevent the "Control Council" or the "Administrator" or any other individuals from gaining control of this United Nations Peace Force. But the record shows that the Communists have proved past masters in the art of gaining control of almost any organization which could serve their purposes, even where they represented a small minority. A well-organized minority always is stronger than a disorganized majority, and as the Communists have been quite successful in infiltrating even originally patriotic and nonpolitical organizations, they have managed to establish "cells" of comrades who, because of their rigid discipline and single-mindedness of purpose, eventually wrested control of these organizations from the unsuspecting majority.

Using this well-proven scheme, the Soviets would doubtless make every effort to gradually and inconspicuously gain control of the international police force. If they should succeed in doing so, despite all agreements and stipulations to the contrary, they would have a tailor-made tool for achieving exactly what they have set out to achieve—establishment of a global military dictatorship. And they could achieve it without cost, without effort and without fighting for it because the only nation which could possibly challenge them, the United States, would be "generally and completely" disarmed and, therefore, impotent to resist take-over by a Communist-controlled and heavily armed "international" police force.

I am by no means the first or only one to express concern about the prospect that one nation or group may use an international police force for its own purposes. Ironically enough, it was none other than ex-Dictator Khrushchev who voiced a similar concern—although in a different context—several years ago. He said, "The imperialists want to build up a kind of international police force which would be virtually under the control of the United States and be used to suppress the peoples who have risen against colonial slavery. This will not succeed!"

There is no sense in wasting time to disprove this ridiculous accusation because our record speaks for itself. But the Soviet and Communist record speaks for itself also, and it says loud and clear that the Soviets, aided by their allies, would make a determined effort and, as likely as not, manage to gain control of any international police force.

Another serious risk stems from the Soviets' infamous record of broken treaties and agreements. Any worldwide effort designed to achieve complete disarmament and eventual world government must be based on strict adherence to a series of complex treaties which can be enforced only as long as a majority of the parties concerned want them enforced. Judging from past experience, it is certain that the Soviets would obstruct such enforcement whenever this would be to their advantage.

The Soviets have made it clear that they would always support the type of aggression which Khrushchev cynically termed "National Wars of Liberation." Hence any international peace organization or world government would be powerless to stop Communist aggression anywhere in the world because the Soviets, backed by their satellites and many "newly emerged" nations, would vote against enforcement of treaty provisions for halting any act of aggression which would serve their cause. In fact, the Soviets would not even need a majority in the proposed "Control Council" or any other governing body because they would insist on retaining the veto right which they have used so liberally and destructively in the Security Council of the United Nations. Moreover, they would doubtless encourage and assist the aggressors, as they have always done in the past.

Nor would there be any assurance that the Soviets would actually disarm in accordance with the treaty provisions, regardless of any inspection system that may be devised. The "Blueprint for the Peace Race" provides for the retention of agreed upon national police forces. It is self-understood that the United States and its Western allies would actually maintain only such forces and equipment as required to uphold internal law and order. However, the Soviets could—and surely would —use this as a subterfuge to give military training to large numbers of men through rapid turnover of their allotted police forces, just as the Nazis did after World War I—under the very eyes of the allied inspectors.

The only safeguard in any type of treaty or agreement is mutual trust and good faith. The Soviets have given us no reason to trust them, and they have rarely if ever exhibited good faith in their dealings with us or any other nation. We can still resist their trickery and blackmail because, so far, we have retained military superiority over them. But this would change radically if we were to scrap our weapons and dismantle our defense industry, entrusting our future fate and survival to the whims of a Communist-controlled world government. We would be utterly defenseless against any military forces directed or surreptitiously maintained by the Communists if the Soviets should decide to break or abrogate the treaties holding the world government together. As the recent examples of Berlin, Cuba, Cyprus and Panama—to name but a few—have shown, even treaties entered into in good faith at the time can and will be abrogated unilaterally as conditions or governments change.

Another threat to a world government is posed by the aggressive intentions of Communist China. There is little doubt that Red China would never submit to the mandate of an International Disarmament Organization, as proposed in the "Blueprint for the Peace Race," nor to the rule of a world government. With 700 million people, one-quarter of the world's population, it is under the absolute control of fanatic and ruthless dictators who are determined to conquer all of southeast Asia. Their newly gained nuclear capability is still limited, but once they have succeeded in building up a sufficient stockpile of nuclear weapons and delivery vehicles they will doubtless embark on a major and sustained campaign of aggression against their neighbors. What would those nations which would have joined the world government and disarmed under its charter do about that? Some might suggest sending China stiff notes of indignant protest; others might go so far as to recommend use of the United Nations Peace Force; but some would actually support Red China in its "National War of Liberation," to use Mr. Khrushchev's definition of Communist aggression. In the end, any type of world government would prove its impotence in dealing with this and any other major acts of aggression and fall apart, with the disarmed United States and its Western allies left to pick up the pieces.

These are but a few of the seldom mentioned risks and problems entailed in "general and complete" disarmament and one-world government. But despite the risks and the price involved, the one-world syndrome persists and flourishes. The symptoms are unmistakable and they are everywhere, even in the highest circles of government. The very submission of the "Blueprint for the Peace Race" is indicative of the official support of disarmament and the unavoidable surrender of more and more of our national rights to an international organization. This is further indicated by the 1963 "Treaty for a Partial Nuclear Test Ban" and, especially, its Preamble, which includes this statement:

> Proclaiming as their principal aim the speediest possible achievement of an agreement on general and complete disarmament under strict international control in accordance with the objectives of the United Nations. . . .

Other indicators include this nation's avowed willingness to halt the production of nuclear armaments; to destroy nuclear weapons carriers on a quid-pro-quo basis; to renounce the use of space for military purposes, even for defense; to permit our strategic strike capability, the keystone of our deterrent posture, to erode; and many others.

Also disquieting is the complacency of so many of our citizens who fail to recognize the one-world syndrome and, if they do, fail to understand its implications. Conversely, the proponents of disarmament and one-world government promote their cause aggressively and relentlessly. Some of them go so far as to advocate unilateral disarmament "as a means of persuasion," naïvely expecting that if we would just go ahead and disarm anyway, the Soviets and their vassals would be "persuaded" to do likewise! One fanatic supporter of the "peace race" even suggested that persons accused of "crime against peace" should be executed and that "any and all Americans should be deputized to try and execute the sentence."

Like any other aggressive ideology, one-worldism has its share of fanatics, extremists and lunatics. But the bulk of the advocates of disarmament and world government is composed of serious and intelligent men who sincerely believe that theirs is the only possible and desirable solution to the problem of survival in the nuclear age. I am confident that the majority of the American people will disagree with them and continue to support our national policy of deterrence as the only acceptable solution to the problem of *national* survival. And that is the subject to which I want to address myself now.

6. Deterrence Dilemma

LET us assume that, in 1941, the United States had possessed nuclear weapons as well as a large fleet of long-range bombers and hundreds of Intercontinental Ballistic Missiles—in other words, the weapons which it has today. Let us further assume that Germany and Japan had the weapons which they actually did possess at that particular time—airplanes with the speed and range possible in the 1940s, manually controlled antiaircraft artillery and, above all, only non-nuclear "conventional" munitions.

Under these conditions, it would have been ridiculous for Nazi Germany or Japan to even dream of challenging the United States. The attack on Pearl Harbor would have been unthinkable because the Japanese warlords would have known that we could have destroyed their entire country overnight and with absolute impunity. World War II would have never been risked by Hitler if we had threatened to intervene, because he would have been certain of losing it disastrously.

The point I am trying to make is that military superiority *can* deter aggression and prevent war, provided it is convincing enough and is used effectively as a diplomatic tool. This concept has been the basis of our national policy of deterrence since the end of World War II. But while this policy has been successful in preventing another world war to this date, conditions have changed so radically that it has become necessary to reappraise thoroughly the application and, indeed, the continued feasibility of our deterrent policy. As a result, there is not only growing opposition to that policy but also wide disagreement among those who support it at least in principle.

It is essential that the American people familiarize themselves with the issues involved because this controversy is neither purely academic, as it may appear on the surface, nor of interest only to the civilian and military strategists. Its outcome will have a profound impact on the future of this nation, and since it will determine the size and character of our military establishment, will affect every American both as a citizen and a taxpayer.

Starting out from the premise that, at least for some time to come, this nation will continue to pursue a policy of deterrence, we must ask ourselves three pertinent questions. First, exactly what is "deterrence" and whom or what are we trying to deter? Second, what types of deterrence are there and which of these types should we choose in order to accomplish our objectives? Third, what actions are necessary to implement the type of deterrence we select?

To "deter" means to "restrain or discourage from action through fear of consequences." This basic principle is as old as man himself, but I do not believe that there is any precedent in history for its application to national policy for the sole purpose of maintaining a fair and just peace. We initiated this policy after World War II when the United States emerged as the most powerful nation on earth and was thrust into the role of guardian of the newly won peace. The military might of our two most powerful adversaries, Germany and Japan, had been thoroughly broken. Soviet Russia then was our ally, and although we did not approve of its Communist regime and dictatorship, it seemed quite unlikely that it would pose a real threat to anyone in the foreseeable future. It had been hurt so badly in World War II and was industrially so backward that it could not possibly challenge us for many years to come—or so we thought.

In contrast to our enemies and many of our allies we had suffered very little. Our cities were unscathed; our casualties, however deplorable, represented only a small percentage of our population; our economy and industry were booming. And despite the headlong dismantling of our war industry and military establishment, we remained militarily far superior to any other nation on earth, primarily because of the newly organized Strategic Air Command. SAC, as it came to be known, was the only force in the world equipped with atomic bombs, and it had enough heavy bombardment aircraft to carry both atomic and conventional bombs to any trouble spot on the globe. The results of our massive bombing attacks were still very much in evidence, and the memory of the atom-bomb attacks on Nagasaki and Hiroshima was still fresh. Thus, the mere existence of SAC, with its bombers and atomic weapons, served as a most effective deterrent to any aggressive move against this country or its allies.

Indeed, our role as guardians of the peace was an easy one during those early postwar years. In fact, our economic, industrial and military superiority was so overwhelming that we could have readily imposed our will and domination on the rest of the world. Nothing could have been further from our minds; instead, we used our strength and wealth to help other countries, friend and foe alike, to recover from the ravages of World War II. In 1947 Congress approved the "Marshall Plan," which provided economic aid amounting to some $12 billion to European countries and set the pattern for similar assistance programs. Without these programs the fantastic postwar recovery and economic rise of the countries thus aided would have been impossible.

But our foreign-aid programs soon had to go beyond the original purpose of speeding postwar recovery. Also in 1947, President Truman asked Congress for $400 million to assist Greece and Turkey both economically and militarily in combating

Communism. This and many subsequent foreign-aid programs became necessary in order to meet a new threat to world peace, namely, the rapidly growing threat of Communist aggression. For despite the losses it had suffered and its immense internal problems, the Soviet Union already had embarked on its global campaign toward the Communist goal of world domination, using every trick in the Communist book—subversion, broken treaties, propaganda, military interference, and a preposterous amount of pure bluff—to achieve its objectives.

In the early 1950s our military position was still so superior that we could have crushed Communism at its root, despite the vast inroads it had made all over the world, especially on the Chinese mainland. Perhaps our last chance came in October 1956 when the Hungarian people revolted against their Communist oppressors. The Soviets still were not strong enough to risk war with the United States although they had exploded their first hydrogen device some three years earlier. If we had intervened in the Hungarian revolt—or merely threatened to intervene—I think we would have called the Soviets' bluff and forced them to withdraw their hordes and vassals from Hungary, permitting the Hungarian people to establish a democratic government. The whole Free World would have applauded our action; in fact, it was expected of us. Other satellite nations would have been encouraged to follow the example of Hungary, and Communism would have been dealt a perhaps fatal blow.

But we chose not to intervene in Hungary. We did not try to quickly end and win the war in Korea. When the Soviets established a land blockade of West Berlin in 1948, we did not attempt to break the blockade by force but resorted to the peaceful airlift to supply the beleaguered city. I believe that, in all these and many other cases, we could have made more effective use of our then still vastly superior military strength and done so with relative impunity and certain success. It is academic to reflect whether, in the long run, we have done a greater service to the cause of freedom and democracy by listening to the voices of restraint and caution, or whether we should have used every opportunity to crush Communist aggression—as long as we had such opportunity. Only the historians, many years from now, will be able to decide whether we did right or not.

But be it as it may, our national policy of countering Communist aggression and expansionism had become essentially defensive in nature. This was reflected in our military strategy which continued to emphasize deterrence but was now directed primarily against the Soviet Union, the only nation posing a direct and expanding military threat. We countered this threat with an even more formidable one, namely, the threat of retaliating any attack on this country or its allies with utter destruction of Russia's rebuilt or newly built cities and industry. This was called the concept of "massive retaliation" and remained the keystone of our deterrent strategy throughout most of the 1950s.

Although much maligned and criticized, even by people in our own camp, the threat of massive retaliation proved instrumental in discouraging the Soviets from waging open aggression against any of our allies, let alone this country, and also helped strengthen the hand of our statesmen in resisting Communist blackmail. There could be no doubt that we were fully prepared and capable of carrying out our threat of massive retaliation if compelled to do so. This was the specific mission of the Strategic Air Command, which continued to increase its striking power in the face of the Soviets' rapidly growing military strength.

In the meantime, however, a number of events and developments had taken place which gradually modified the concept of massive retaliation. Foremost among them was the Soviets' spectacular buildup of a nuclear capability which now matches ours in some respects and, in the field of very high-yield nuclear weapons, even surpasses it. Equally ominous is the Soviets' large, and probably still growing, stockpile of Intermediate-Range and Intercontinental Ballistic Missiles which, supported by their long-range bombers and missile-firing submarines, can subject this country and its allies to a devastating nuclear surprise attack. Directly related to these factors is the popular thesis that this country and the Soviet Union have reached a "nuclear stalemate" (which some people in the Western world consider desirable for the sake of peace) and that, as a result, the Soviets would limit military aggression to "brushfire wars" with which we should be better prepared to deal.

Other factors which must be considered in shaping our military strategy and policy for the future include the possibility, and indeed likelihood, of Soviet offensive weapons in space; the possible development of revolutionary new and yet undreamed-of weapons; the mounting cost of the so-called "arms race," that is, our effort to stay ahead of the Soviets technologically and militarily; the emergence of Communist China as a nuclear power; the proliferation of nuclear capability, that is, the acquisition of nuclear weapons and missiles by small nations; and the military demands of the cold war.

It is, therefore, evident that as the threat to the nation's survival grew more complex and assumed many faces, the simple expedient of countering every aspect of that threat with the threat of massive retaliation was no longer adequate. Consequently, it had to yield to a more sophisticated approach designed to permit greater flexibility and selectivity in the application of our strategic strike forces. In fact, military power in general had become only one of several cold-war tools and now is part of a broad, overall deterrent that must be responsive to a wide variety of contingencies.

In order to develop a deterrent strategy which is as effective as the concept of massive retaliation had been in the past but dynamic enough to serve all present and future needs, a number of conditions must be met. These conditions include the requirement for "adequate" strategic forces which are always and instantly ready, even after the losses sustained in a surprise attack, to exact an "unacceptable" price from any aggressor. And this is where most of the disagreement and controversy come in. While there is general agreement that the objective of any deterrent strategy is to prevent nuclear war and maintain an "honorable" peace, there is no agreement at all on what constitutes an "unacceptable" price for aggression and the "adequate" military force structure needed to exact such a price under any and all conditions.

Both experienced and self-appointed strategists by the dozen have written and spoken millions of words on this vital subject and promulgated a variety of deterrent theories with such appealing names as "Finite Deterrence," "Graduated Deterrence," "Counterforce Deterrence" and, last but not least, "Minimum Deterrence." The proponents of each of these and other deterrent theories advocate a different strategy and, as a rule, a different military force structure with different weapon systems and tactics for implementing their pet strategy. As far as the public is concerned, all this is very confusing; in fact, the average citizen could not care less—except that he will have to pay for whatever force structure is decided upon and that he or his children may lose everything if whatever deterrent theory may be selected should prove a failure.

Without going into the fine points of all these theories, it may be well to discuss the general characteristics of the most popular ones. As indicated by official pronouncements and actions in the recent past, the current trend appears to be toward a "city-busting" deterrent which is the basic premise of both the Minimum Deterrent and the Finite Deterrent. The principle is to maintain in instant readiness a large number of ballistic missiles, both in hardened and widely dispersed sites on land and in prowling Polaris submarines at sea, which would be launched against Russian cities should the Soviets attack us. The advocates of this principle are convinced that the threatened destruction of many or most of their large population centers would effectively deter the Soviets from starting or risking general nuclear war.

The main difference between the concepts of Minimum Deterrence and Finite Deterrence lies in the number of cities that would have to be targeted. Minimum Deterrence advocates the "minimum necessary" number because it reasons that if the threatened destruction of, say, fifty cities cannot deter nuclear war, five or ten times that number cannot accomplish this purpose either. Finite Deterrence calls for a larger or finite number of city targets because of the conviction that nothing short of the threat of a crippling blow can be an adequate deterrent.

In my opinion, all variations of the "city-busting" deterrent have in common some major weaknesses; and one fundamental fallacy which makes their effectiveness as deterrents to nuclear aggression questionable, at best. This fallacy is the assumption that we know what will deter the Soviets (and, eventually, the Chinese or any other Johnny-come-latelies in the nuclear arena) from achieving their avowed objectives through nuclear aggression, once all other methods have failed. Let us take a good look at some historical facts and figures, and see whether we can apply our concept of "unacceptable" losses, damage or price to that of the Soviets.

When we think of major catastrophes this country has suffered, there may come to mind the great Chicago fire in 1871 or the San Francisco earthquake in 1906. In the one, 250 people died and 452 in the other. Our worst peacetime disaster in terms of human lives was the Galveston hurricane in 1900 in which some 5,000 persons perished.

However appalling to us, these figures would not impress the average Russian. About two million people succumbed to the typhus epidemic which ravaged Russia after World War I. An estimated three million Russians died in the disastrous famine during the early 1920s. And Stalin's ruthless collectivization is believed to have cost the lives of as many as five million peasants.

There is a similar disparity in wartime losses. While uncounted millions of Russians have been killed in their past wars, the largest number of fatalities suffered in the history of this country was some 600,000—the deaths resulting from our Civil War. Fifteen times more Russians than Americans died in World War I. We lost less than 300,000 men in World War II which cost the Russians about 7.5 million military and 12.5 million civilian dead.

Thus, tradition and experience have conditioned the Russians to accept catastrophic losses in lives that would seem unacceptable to us. This fatalistic attitude, coupled with the utter lack of morals and scruples exhibited by the Soviet rulers, may account for the inhuman manner in which huge numbers of Russians have been slaughtered by their own countrymen.

The Soviets' savage purges reached their climax under Joseph Stalin, whose insane lust for power knew no mercy in "liquidating" Communist and non-Communist Russians alike. Among his bloodiest purges was the infamous "police action" in the Ukraine after World War II which was masterminded by one of his most loyal henchmen—one Nikita Khrushchev, later to become his successor and defamer. The world will probably never know how many Russian lives were sacrificed throughout the evolution of Sovietism, but indicative of their number is the estimate that over 750,000 alone were slain during Stalin's purges of the 1930s.

With such grisly tradition and shocking record in the massacre of their own people, the Soviets cannot be expected to let the risk of even millions of Russian lives deter them from starting a nuclear war if they should consider such a war to be in the best interests of the Communist cause. Nor would they be deterred by the danger of losing some cities because widespread devastation and subsequent recovery have had numerous precedents in Russia's hectic history.

During my visit to Russia with General Twining, we were given an interesting briefing by some of the officers who had participated in the great battle of Stalingrad, later renamed "Volgograd" by ex-Stalinist Khrushchev. Hitler's hordes, in an attempt to cross the Volga, had occupied the northern part of the city but were stopped in their drive and, eventually, decisively defeated. Honored as one of Russia's "Hero Cities," Stalingrad was almost completely destroyed and depopulated. To rebuild this vital port and industrial center, the Soviets resorted to a very effective expedient. As our hosts explained it to us, they had their architects draw up a master plan, handed it to the people of Stalingrad as they were returning to the ruins of their city, and told them: "Build it!" And the citizens of Stalingrad built it; it was as simple as that.

There was no need for making loans or floating bond issues, nor for worrying about labor and materials. The people just went ahead and did exactly as they were told. By 1950, Stalingrad had regained its prewar population. Today, what is now known as Volgograd is a very beautiful and modern city with a population of close to 600,000 and still growing. Its busy factories line the banks of the Volga for miles, and an entirely new industrial city, Volzhski, has arisen across the river.

Or take the city of Magnitogorsk, prototype of the new Soviet industrial centers. It was founded in 1931, on the left bank of the Ural River and on the western slope of the magnetite-rich Magnitnaya Mountain for which it was named. Huge blast and open-hearth furnaces, steel rolling mills, coke batteries, and numerous other industries sprang up from nothing. By 1939, the city's population was already close to 150,000. Less than ten years later, that figure had more than doubled. Today, Magnitogorsk is Russia's leading metallurgical center and produces much of its steel—most of it going into armaments.

Magnitogorsk is but one of many similar remarkable developments which started from scratch or started from very little—like Stalinsk. With only the small town of Kuznetsk across the Tom River, Stalinsk was founded in 1929, soon to become another industrial key city in the Soviet Union. Boasting a population of over 350,000 by 1960, it now accounts for a sizable percentage of Russia's aluminum and steel production.

Indeed, the Soviets would probably consider the mere loss of a number of cities as an acceptable price for a decisive victory over the United States. For they know from experience that it would not take them long to rebuild a bombed-out city as they rebuilt Stalingrad and, if persistent radioactivity should present a problem, to build a brand-new city somewhere else in their vast country as they built Magnitogorsk, Stalinsk and many others.

The point is that what will deter us will not necessarily deter the Soviets, and what will make them accept risks will not make us accept similar risks. Moral principles, and the danger to American lives and cities would deter us strongly from launching a pre-emptive war unless there were no other way of averting certain aggression and still greater losses. But moral considerations and the prospect of losing Russian lives and cities would not deter the Soviets from launching an aggressive war if they saw no better way of achieving their objectives.

These distinctions must be borne in mind in trying to determine the degree of deterrence required to discourage Communist aggression. No nation—or dictatorship in full control of a nation—will intentionally start a war unless it is confident that the gains to be derived from this war will outweigh its cost, thus ensuring a reasonable profit. Hence, we can hope to deter Communist aggression only so long as we manage to keep the Soviets convinced that, even measured by their standards, the gains would be far too small and the cost far too high to make aggression against the United States or its allies profitable.

Our problem, then, is to ascertain exactly what the Soviets would consider "unprofitable" and what is required of us to keep them convinced that aggression would gain them less and cost more than they would be willing to accept. Unfortunately, there are no conclusive answers to these important questions because the concept of deterrence is not only very complex but also very flexible and subject to many factors which change from day to day. Moreover, little would be gained by trying to deter the Russian people; the ones to be deterred are the very few who are in full control of the Russian people.

Offhand, the small number of men involved and the authority they wield may seem to simplify the problem of deterrence. If one command from them can set off a nuclear war, it can also defer war for any length of time, perhaps indefinitely. And it certainly should be easier to deal with a small and fairly stable group of strong men than with a weak and unstable government or with millions of antagonistic people.

It must be remembered, however, that the Soviet rulers themselves are, in effect, merely tools of the system which gave them their power, and that they have no choice but to comply with its unequivocal demands—ruthless pursuit of the Communist objectives. No deterrent, however imposing, will sway their determination to achieve these objectives but can affect only their decision of *how* and *when* to achieve them.

To fight their way to the top in the Soviet hierarchy and to protect both their positions and health in this dynamite-laden atmosphere takes men with minds, hearts and nerves of steel. Men of this type and caliber are not easily deterred from anything or by anything—except that which threatens them personally. And here lies the one weakness in the Communist system which makes our policy of deterrence feasible. We can deter the Soviet rulers from attacking the United States so long as we can keep them convinced that aggression and subsequent nuclear war would endanger their collective leadership, their individual ambitions, and their personal security.

The members of the Soviet hierarchy are not starving fanatics or religious zealots. In addition to their unprecedented power, they command immense wealth and have absolute privacy to do with their wealth as they please. In fact, very few people even know—or would dare investigate—where and how they spend their private lives.

It stands to reason that men enjoying such riches—not to mention the fabulous privileges that go with their high offices —have no greater fear than to lose all this and, possibly, their lives besides. To protect themselves against this ominous contingency, the members of the Communist elite must do a number of things. They must endeavor to keep their superiors satisfied that they are not scheming for their positions. They must keep on guard against the men behind them who are scheming for *their* positions. And, finally, they must keep their associates and the hierarchy as a whole convinced that they are of continued value to the Communist cause.

The worst crime of which a Soviet functionary can be accused, apart from disloyalty to the Party or his superiors, is failure to accomplish his assignment, regardless of whether such failure is his personal fault, the fault of his subordinates or that of the system. As, by definition, the system can never fail, someone must take the blame and consequences.

For this reason, the top Soviet chiefs do not like to take a gamble unless they are confident that the odds are heavily in their favor or can be turned to their favor. This characteristic of the professional gambler has guided most of the Soviets' decisions and would undoubtedly also guide the decision of whether and when to start a war against the United States. The Communist doctrine does not spell out specifically that its ends must be accomplished by war or military force, but it does demand that the most expeditious and effective means, including war, must be used in furthering the Party's objectives.

Considering all these factors, it should be clear that once the Soviets have reached the conclusion that they cannot attain their objectives without a war against the United States, their decision to start the war will be based on a careful assessment of their strengths and our weaknesses. Their conclusions must satisfy two conditions before they can afford to initiate aggression. First, there must be adequate assurance that the war will result in a decisive victory for them and unconditional surrender on our part. Any result short of this goal—even an indecisive stalemate—would have to be regarded as a failure, and the man or group responsible for this failure would have to pay for it dearly.

Therefore, one major aspect of deterrence lies in our continued ability to keep the Soviet rulers in doubt that their attack would succeed and that the ensuing nuclear war would yield the desired results. Toward this end, we need not only an effective military defense system but also an equally effective civil defense establishment, backed by thorough preparations for rapid recovery from a nuclear surprise attack.

The second condition that must be satisfied before the Soviet rulers would undertake aggression against the United States is the assurance that they can prevent our retaliatory counterattack from inflicting "unacceptable damage" upon them. Vague terms such as "unacceptable damage" and "decisive results" permit, of course, of broad interpretation. For the reasons explained previously, we must use a different yardstick in trying to gauge the Soviets' concept of "unacceptable" than we would use if we were to plan a pre-emptive war against them. But despite their callousness and disrespect for the masses' welfare, the Soviet rulers cannot risk losses that might preclude continuation of the war once they had started it or, if they should win it, might relegate the Soviet Union to a second-rate power.

An added problem is the reaction of the Russian people. There can be no doubt that, in a nuclear war, they would accept heavy losses without protest so long as they believed that the United States, not Russia, was responsible for the war. But once it dawned on them that the war had resulted from Soviet aggression, and their losses would continue to mount, the point might possibly be reached where neither fear of reprisal nor the remnants of the police forces could stop the masses from rebelling against their rulers.

For all these reasons, it is highly unlikely that the Soviet leaders would accept the loss of an *unlimited* number of Russian lives and cities as the price of nuclear aggression. Obviously, they must have some limits for the degree and type of damage they can accept without endangering their regime, the objectives of the Communist doctrine, and the already embattled position of the Soviet Union within the Communist empire.

The problem is that we will never be able to ascertain exactly what these limits are, for the simple reason that the Soviet rulers themselves may not know and, even if they did, might change their minds from one day to the other, depending on the circumstances and the caliber of the men in control of the Party at any particular time.

Some of the men who dominate the Party at present are old revolutionaries whom many years of bitter struggle, age and success have mellowed, at least to the extent where they have become more cautious and wily. They are like old-time gangsters who have amassed vast fortunes and power and, hiding behind a front of cozy respectability, have grown less inclined to take undue risks. Similarly, the old Bolsheviks still alive and in power may have a lower limit for the price of aggression today than they might have been willing to accept in their earlier days.

But the time will come before too long when this generation will die out and another generation will assume the leadership of the Party and the Soviet drive toward world domination. Whoever these men will be, they will know little of the bloody struggles of the Communist Revolution but, from their earliest youth, will have been thoroughly indoctrinated in the precepts and demands of the Communist creed. Hence, they can be expected to be far more aggressive and reckless than their aging predecessors in pursuing the ultimate Communist objectives. They may not be satisfied with the slow progress made through cold-war tactics and favor a radical and quick solution through decisive military action—even if it would entail all-out nuclear war—setting a much higher limit for "acceptable" price than the present older Soviet rulers would consider.

(A still higher price would certainly be accepted by the rulers of Communist China once they have achieved the capability to wage nuclear aggression. One of them reportedly has stated that Red China could lose half its population in a nuclear war and still remain the most populous nation on earth. He was speaking of sacrificing the lives of some 350 million people!)

Nor is the limit of "acceptable damage" the only variable in the deterrent equation; there may also be profound changes in relative military strength or its assessment by potential aggressors. As I mentioned earlier, Minimum or Finite Deterrence, as envisioned today, is based essentially on an "adequate" number of ballistic missiles—SAC ICBMs on land and the Navy's Polaris missiles at sea—which are poised to be launched against major Russian cities and population centers in case of nuclear aggression. But what would happen if the Soviets should succeed in developing an effective antimissile defense or are led to *believe* that they have an effective defense against our missiles? Obviously, much if not all of our deterrent would go down the drain!

Even if the Soviets should fail in developing an impenetrable antimissile defense, I am certain that they can and will strive for vast superiority in missile numbers which, coupled with dramatic increases in missile accuracy, would promise them a high mathematical probability of destroying most or all of our hardened and dispersed ICBMs before they could be launched in retaliation.

A deterrent equation based primarily on missiles could be further upset in the Soviets' favor by other future developments, such as methods for detecting and destroying our Polaris submarines, and weapons in space. The Soviets may already have the capability—and certainly will have eventually—to place in space and over our heads nuclear weapons of very high yield, perhaps as much as 100 megatons which is the equivalent of 100 million tons of TNT. We do not know what the detonation of such a tremendous weapon will do to the operability and performance of our ICBMs in their silos below, and we will never find out as long as we are prevented from testing in the atmosphere. But chances are that the Soviets know, because they have tested nuclear weapons of far higher yields than we have.

Under these circumstances it appears quite unrealistic to entrust our future survival to a highly elusive and hypothetical Minimum Deterrent, especially one depending essentially on missiles. Yet, the proponents of Minimum or Finite Deterrence have a very appealing case. They maintain that their deterrent concept is the most economical one of all; that it will slow the arms race; that it is not provocative; and, above all, that it will make nuclear war impossible and, therefore, permit us to direct our attention and efforts to the resolution of limited conflicts.

It should be evident, however, that all these advantages would prevail only under one condition, namely, that the Minimum Deterrent or any similar concept will achieve its purpose, effectively and indefinitely. As I tried to show, this seems very unlikely, and therefore I do not recommend it. Conversely, we could go to the other extreme and choose what is sometimes called the "Maximum Deterrent." In other words, we could devote our entire economy and industry to the establishment of a military potential of such fantastic proportions that no aggressor in his right mind would ever dare challenge it. This I do not recommend either because such an effort, as I put it earlier, would destroy economically what we are trying to preserve militarily. Most importantly, there is no need for a Maximum Deterrent to deter aggression and prevent nuclear war.

It stands to reason that the optimum deterrent must lie somewhere between the illusory minimum and the impossible maximum. Several deterrent concepts have been advanced which are based on this premise. For instance, there is the concept of "Counterforce Deterrence" which places greater importance on saving American lives than on destroying an aggressor's cities. Its strategy calls for deterring aggression by building a strike force that is directed strictly against and capable of defeating the enemy's military forces, the cardinal principle being that the United States should never attack an enemy city unless the enemy has first attacked an American city. The supporters of Counterforce Deterrence realize that any deterrent may fail and they maintain that, for this reason, any deterrent strategy based entirely on the threat of city destruction entails the risk of losing many millions of American lives. They call the concept of Finite or "City-Busting" Deterrence the "lunacy of mutual annihilation" and submit that "deterrence through avowed resort to mutual suicide is morally and militarily indefensible."

Like other deterrent philosophies, Counterforce Deterrence has much appeal and also serious weaknesses. As it is unlikely that, in a nuclear war, the United States would ever be in a role other than that of retaliation or "second strike," strike forces designed primarily to meet the purposes of Counterforce Deterrence would be of limited value in case deterrence should fail. They may help deter but they could not prevent a devastating surprise attack on this country and, after such an attack, presumably would seek to destroy primarily the enemy's residual restrike capability.

In the unlikely case that the United States should start a nuclear war against the Soviet Union, the Counterforce strike forces could undoubtedly make effective use of their inherent "first-strike" capability and limit the Soviet's retaliatory potential. I am not convinced, however, that any pre-emptive attack on our part, which would concentrate on known and fixed military targets, could prevent or deter the Soviets from using their remaining strike capability to mount retaliatory attacks against our cities.

In my opinion, the main weakness of the concept of Counterforce Deterrence lies in the assumption that if we do not attack Soviet cities, the Soviets will not attack ours. This weakness is recognized by the advocates of "Graduated Deterrence" which, in effect, is a compromise between Finite and Counterforce Deterrence. It calls for the capability to destroy those population centers which are of major strategic significance as well as fixed military installations (control centers, airfields, missiles sites, and the like).

The supporters of Graduated Deterrence, perhaps even more than those of Minimum and Finite Deterrence, consider the problems of limited war far more pressing than those of general nuclear war. They maintain that, being unable to destroy each other's counterforces *and* being unwilling to risk destruction of their cities, both sides will endeavor to limit hostilities to local conflicts and fight them with conventional weapons in order to prevent their expansion into all-out nuclear war.

Variations of these philosophies call for "flexible response," which is the capability to retaliate in kind; that is, to go after Russian cities if the Soviets attack ours or to limit our retaliatory attack on Soviet military installations if their initial attack is directed only against our military installations. Another variation emphasizes "damage-limiting" capability, which calls for a strategy designed to concentrate on those targets in the aggressor's territory which pose a direct threat to American population centers and industrial complexes.

As can be seen, the "deterrence dilemma" is very real, especially since the supporters of each of the many deterrence concepts and their variations insist that theirs is the only feasible one and argue their cause with much persuasion and appeal. But all these theories, in my opinion, are highly unrealistic because they have in common one fundamental deficiency—they fail to take into account a credible assessment of the threat and any possible changes in the nature and scope of that threat.

I submit that it is futile to try to meet any threat without an objective and adequate assessment of what it entails. I realize that because of the unprecedented complexity and ever changing nature of the threat to our survival—and I am speaking now only of the military threat—such an assessment is most difficult, and it becomes, therefore, largely a matter of judgment. And that is where the problem lies. All persons concerned, in one way or another, with the formulation of our military strategy have available to them all the information and intelligence data that can be obtained. Yet while they have the same information, they interpret it differently and, as a result, arrive at different conclusions.

The reason for the perplexing differences in the evaluation of identical information is very simple. If a person believes very strongly in one of the above described deterrent philosophies which calls for a lesser U. S. military posture, his judgment and assessment of the present and future threat will be colored or tempered by that belief. Conversely, if a person adheres to a philosophy which demands a stronger military posture, his judgment will be affected accordingly.

My personal belief is that we really know too little of the Soviets' total military capabilities and exact intentions to arrive at a conclusive judgment on which to base a well-defined and rigid deterrent strategy for the future. Even if we could get complete and accurate information on the Soviets' military posture, order of battle and war plans—which, of course, is impossible—we still would not know what their plans are for the next two or five or ten years. And even if we would know, we still could not be certain that they would actually follow these plans and not change them radically and suddenly for any number of unpredictable reasons.

We find ourselves in a position similar to that of a man who wants to take out insurance to protect himself against any possible judgment in a civil suit arising from an automobile accident during the coming year. If he were to know the exact amount for which he will be sued throughout the next twelve months, he would be foolish to insure himself for more than that. But he does not know and, therefore, the amount of insurance he will take out becomes entirely a matter of judgment and "assessment of the threat." This is the reason why different people carry different amounts of liability insurance. Some have more to protect than others or place a greater value on what they want to protect. Some are more cautious and pessimistic; others do not care to spend money for insurance and carry little or, perhaps, no insurance at all. It is their choice.

Similarly, the American people must decide what they want to protect, how much it is worth to them, and what kind of protection they desire in order to insure the nation against a threat whose future magnitude and nature are unpredictable. What is at stake is our national survival, and I have no doubt that the majority of our citizens is determined to protect it at all cost. But because of the many uncertainties and variables in the military threat to our survival it is impossible to pick a neatly wrapped deterrent package from the shelf in a bargain basement. Instead, we must make a *general* assessment of the overall threat and, based on that assessment, establish and maintain a deterrent posture which is broad enough to cover all foreseeable contingencies and flexible enough to be responsive to any unpredictable contingencies.

I am confident that such a deterrent posture can be achieved by basing it on a balanced military force structure which is designed to cover the entire spectrum of military operations and in which the emphasis on each element is determined solely by the nature and scope of the particular phase of the threat this element is intended to meet. Once the parameters of a realistic deterrent posture and of the force structure which it requires have been established, then and only then will it be possible to submit to the Congress a readily defensible military budget. I am certain that Congress will appropriate the requested funds as long as its members can be convinced that these funds will serve to provide the best possible long-range deterrent that can be devised.

This approach appears to be the most, and perhaps only, logical one. However, we are not following it. During my last years as Commander in Chief of the Strategic Air Command I could not escape the impression that the military threat is being underestimated and that, as a result, there is a growing tendency toward neglecting or disregarding some of the most ominous aspects of that threat. The appeal of the very elementary and relatively inexpensive "city-busting" deterrent, together with the demands for "cost effectiveness," inter-Service competition for the defense dollar, budgetary limitations, and political expediency, especially during the crucial election year of 1964— all combined to bring about a marked shift to limited-war forces, at the expense of our nuclear deterrent and of the strategic strike forces capable of waging—and deterring—both nuclear and conventional war.

I consider this a very unwise and dangerous approach for it presupposes that we are thoroughly familiar with Soviet capabilities and intentions, which is not at all the case. It could prove a fatal mistake to cut back the most vital component of our military deterrent because of an arbitrary judgment that stems from a subjective assessment and underestimation of the military threat. If future events should show this judgment to be erroneous, it would be too late to do anything about it. The long lead times involved in obtaining the necessary hardware and in implementing the military programs would make it impossible to rebuild an adequate and versatile strategic strike capability fast enough, if and when the need to do so should suddenly arise.

For the same reason—the excessive lead times—we are bound always to be years behind the Soviets if we establish our future military programs on the basis of an assessment of what we believe to be their current capabilities and current intentions and current plans. If they should decide to change those intentions and plans, we would find ourselves totally unprepared for whatever they may throw against us and, at best, would have to keep revising our military programs in the hope that the Soviets will not change their mind again and permit us eventually to catch up with them.

Our main problem is that we are cast basically in a retaliatory role, which means that the Soviets have the choice of when and where and how to strike. Conversely, we can deter them only as long as we can keep them convinced that we are capable and prepared to retaliate decisively whenever, wherever and however they may plan to strike. This is possible only if our military programs are broad and general enough to maintain the deterrent posture which I described, despite the long lead times in the orderly implementation of these programs and regardless of any sudden changes in the Soviets' intentions or plans.

That is why I am so gravely concerned about the persistent reduction in the capability and flexibility of our strategic strike forces which I consider the keystone for deterring any kind of war—nuclear or conventional, big or small. While still Commander in Chief of SAC, I brought this concern repeatedly to the attention of my civilian and military superiors. As I have pointed out to them, the present strength of our deterrent, which has helped to prevent nuclear and general war to this date, is the result of actions taken five and ten years ago. By the same token, the actions which we take today will determine the strength of our deterrent five and ten years from now. If we make the wrong decisions, for any reason whatever, we may invite rather than deter nuclear war, and perish as a people rather than survive as a viable nation.

On the basis of what I have experienced, learned and done during almost four decades of executing and planning military strategy, I am convinced that we can devise and indefinitely maintain an effective deterrent against any kind of aggression, at acceptable cost and risk. But this deterrent must be based on a continuous and factual assessment of the threat and must be designed for no other purpose than to meet that threat.

7. Basic Principles of Deterrence

WHEN we speak of the "threat to the nation's survival," we normally think only of the military threat; that is, aggression and nuclear war. We are apt to forget that there are many phases to that threat—the external threat and the internal threat; the ideological threat and the economic threat; the political threat *and* the military threat.

There is no panacea for meeting all these threats at once because they are quite different in nature. Nevertheless, they are closely interrelated since they are all part, or a result, of one all-inclusive threat: the avowed determination of the Communists to achieve global domination by any means whatever.

Against this background of the overall threat, I want to discuss some of the basic principles involved in dealing with the military phase with which I have been intimately and actively connected ever since World War II. That phase, too, has several aspects which include those pertaining to "hot war" and "cold war," general war and limited war, nuclear war and non-nuclear or "conventional" war. Of all these, I consider the threat of general nuclear war the overriding one.

There is much disagreement regarding the methods and strategies we should employ to prevent general nuclear war. It is difficult for the average citizen to judge the respective merits of all these methods and strategies because only one of them has ever been put into practice, and that is the method of deterrence we have used to this date. This method has proved successful, and considering what is at stake, I can only suggest that we stick to a proven formula instead of turning to untried theories, regardless of their alleged promise.

Actually, the reason why there has been no general nuclear war so far is a very simple one—we have not been merely as strong as or a little stronger than the Soviets; we have had overwhelming military superiority. Although the Soviets have managed to whittle down what I call our "deterrent margin"—the scope and degree of our military superiority—I am confident that we can maintain that deterrent margin large enough to prevent general nuclear war indefinitely and on our terms. However, to do so as successfully in the future as we have done in the past, we must follow a few basic principles which I do not think are always well understood.

There are, in particular, two primary principles which I consider so essential to our deterrent posture that I want to discuss them in some detail. The first and, in my opinion, foremost principle is to maintain a *credible* capability to achieve a *military* victory under any set of conditions and circumstances. The second basic principle is to make certain that the Soviets and any other potential aggressors *know* at all times that we have that capability.

Turning first to Principle Number One, it is true that, in an all-out nuclear exchange, both sides would suffer such heavy losses that neither side has the prospect of "winning" anything in the commonly accepted sense. But if one side manages to retain sufficient military strength after the nuclear exchange to terminate hostilities on its terms and to force the surrender of the other side, it has gained what is called a "military victory." This is the kind of victory we must always be able to achieve if we want to deter aggression successfully.

The requirement for such a "war-winning" capability is very much contested by the advocates of most deterrent philosophies and is one of the most controversial subjects among students of military strategy in the Free World. The main argument against the principle of war-winning capability is the proposition that no one can "win" a nuclear war and that, for this reason, it is senseless to waste money, men and matériel in trying to achieve that impossible objective.

In my opinion, this rationale misses a crucial point. If the Soviets should ever decide to force general nuclear war upon us, they would do so only if they were certain of winning it. And the very fact that they are preparing themselves to wage such a war is clear indication that, in *their* estimation, it is not at all impossible to achieve a decisive military victory. Hence, our only hope of deterring them from initiating a general nuclear war lies in convincing them that no matter when and how they might start it, *we* would win, not they.

Another popular misconception is the assumption that there is a "nuclear stalemate" and that, as a result, we cannot maintain a sufficient degree of military superiority to give us a credible war-winning capability.

The term "nuclear stalemate" is another one of those misleading clichés used especially to support the logic of "city-busting" deterrence and of similar passive strategies based on a minimum or limited number of ballistic missiles. It is true that we are in a neck-and-neck race with the Soviets for military supremacy and that both of us now have more than enough nuclear capability to theoretically destroy each other, as in the often quoted analogy of two scorpions locked in a bottle. But the facts of the matter are that we have had an unquestionable war-winning capability ever since World War II, and what is more, we still have it today despite the alleged nuclear stalemate. For we are still ahead of the Soviets in *strategic* strike capability which, with all other things being equal, is the decisive factor in gaining a military victory.

We can preserve this critical advantage as long as we maintain the highly flexible and well-coordinated strategic strike forces we have in being today and keep both modernizing and strengthening them as conditions may warrant. Toward that end, we must provide our strategic forces with the varied advanced tools they may need to cope with any future advances in Soviet matériel and techniques. Next, our strategic strike superiority must always be kept large and obvious enough to be *credible.* Finally, the strength and posture of our strategic forces must always remain such that they can accomplish their mission *under any set of conditions and circumstances,* even in the event of a massive Soviet surprise attack with bombers, missiles and, eventually, spacecraft. I have no doubt that if we meet these requirements we can ensure a *lasting* and *decisive* superiority in strategic strike capability, and thereby, a credible war-winning capability.

Putting it differently, no race is ever decided until the goal line is reached, and neither we nor the Soviets have reached it —assured peace in a Free World for us and world domination for the Soviets. If we should ever slacken our pace in the belief that no one can win the race anyway because of the mythical nuclear stalemate, we would make it easy for the Soviets to catch up with us and surpass us all along the line. However, if we keep on forging ahead, gauging our pace by that of the Soviets, we can always stay ahead of them sufficiently to protect our "deterrent margin."

There is one other misconception regarding the principle of maintaining a war-winning capability which I believe needs some clarification. It has been claimed that even if it were possible to sustain such a capability, it would be too expensive from the standpoint of "cost effectiveness" to make it practical. This is not at all the case; in fact, the opposite is true, especially if "cost" is measured in terms of American lives. Let us examine this particular aspect briefly.

If we want to compare the cost effectiveness of the different deterrent methods proposed, we should apply the same basic principle used by commercial ventures, namely, an analysis of expected costs vs. desired profits. In the case of deterrence, "desired profits" should be primarily the number of American lives and those of our allies we expect to save, not the number of Russians we expect to kill if we were forced to retaliate a nuclear attack.

On that basis, strategic strike forces possessing a war-winning capability promise both the safest and largest "profits," for several reasons. First, they provide the most potent and reliable deterrent that can be devised, since they are designed for the most unfavorable case—the threat of a massive Soviet surprise attack and ensuing general nuclear war. Second, the very fact that they represent such a powerful deterrent to general nuclear war makes them equally effective in discouraging the escalation of limited conflicts and even in resolving such conflicts at a minimum loss of life, as will be discussed in the chapter on "The Issues of Limited War."

Last but by no means least, we must take into account the possibility that deterrence may fail for any number of reasons, no matter how potent our deterrent might be. In such a case, strategic strike forces designed to achieve a military victory under any conditions are the only ones that would have the residual strength, facilities and flexibility to seek out and destroy those enemy targets which pose a continuing threat to the lives of our citizens and allies.

This is a most important point, not only in determining "cost effectiveness" but also in evaluating the overall merits of the various deterrent philosophies, together with the specific force structures they call for. Because of preconceived ideas and personal convictions, opinions regarding the possibility of general nuclear war vary widely. However, most of the experts seem to agree that even the most ingenious and powerful deterrent *may* fail.

I have often stated that if man should resort to nuclear war to settle his arguments and differences, mankind will have reached its highest plateau of stupidity. But there is no guaranty that mankind will never reach that plateau, and all we can do is to make this as unlikely as is humanly possible. In my considered opinion, there is no better and surer way of achieving this objective than to keep all potential aggressors convinced that we do have a "credible capability to achieve a military victory under any set of conditions and circumstances"— my Basic Principle Number One.

This brings me to the second basic principle of deterrence—to make certain that the Soviets and any other potential aggressors *know* at all times that we have an assured war-winning capability.

Obviously, it makes little difference what *we* think of our military capability; the only thing that counts in deterrence is what our enemies think of it. Therefore, if we expect to impress anyone with our military strength and thus deter him from harming us or our friends, we must let him know unequivocally what that strength is and how we intend to apply it if he forces us to use it. While all this may seem self-understood, we have not been very sophisticated as a nation in that respect. For that matter, we tend to give more publicity to our weaknesses than to our strengths.

I do not mean to imply that we should hide our failures and weaknesses. By talking them out in public, the people know exactly where they stand and will see to it that the necessary corrective actions are taken. On the other hand, we should not go overboard in belittling our strengths or expose weaknesses that may not even exist. This is not only unwarranted but can be very dangerous in this high-stake game of deterrence, as it may lead to a fateful miscalculation on the part of the Soviets. If their rulers should be led to overestimate their capabilities and underestimate ours, we would have to accept a large share of the blame because, all too often, we help them gain an exaggerated view of both their accomplishments and our weaknesses. In my opinion, this is the surest way of bringing on a miscalculation and encouraging aggression.

A costly experience that should have taught us an object lesson was the miscalculation which led to World War II. Nazi dictator Adolf Hitler had heard innumerable expressions of apparent weakness come from the democratic camps on both sides of the Atlantic. Neville Chamberlain's pleas for peace further strengthened his impression that the allied powers were too weak and afraid to fight. At the same time, he heard the brazen and strong talk that came from his own camp. And he heard his gaudy air force chief, Reich Marshal Hermann Goering, boast of his air defenses: "The Ruhr will not be subjected to a single bomb. If an enemy bomber reaches the Ruhr, my name is not Hermann Goering; you can call me Meier!"

Adding up the strong talk of his people and the weak talk and actions of his intended victims, Hitler became convinced that he could take on the whole Free World. Of course, he was wrong; but it took a world war and untold millions of lives to prove it.

I maintain that we have elements of the same problem today. Undoubtedly, the Soviet rulers hear predominantly favorable reports from their scientists and engineers, because failures are "discouraged." If there are failures—and there are bound to be in any development programs—they are never publicized. Conversely, successes are exploited thoroughly for propaganda purposes. As the Soviets' confidence in their strength continues to mount, we help to boost it further by making their successes as well as our failures often seem more significant than they actually are.

A typical example was the reaction to the announcement of the Soviets' success in placing the first man-made satellite in orbit on October 4, 1957. As was to be expected, this spectacular scientific accomplishment served greatly to inflate the Soviets' ego and confidence factor. At the same time, however, many of our citizens not only acted as if Sputnik had made this country virtually defenseless overnight but also created the impression that our own missile and rocket program was a complete failure. Having been closely associated with this effort, I happened to know that we had a very active program and that it was making gratifying progress despite some unavoidable but widely publicized failures. Still more important, I also knew that Sputnik had not affected our military strength and deterrent in the least and that it was merely a harbinger of what we might have to expect in the future if we did not keep up with the Soviets' advances in space technology.

The almost defeatist reaction of people all over the Free World was impressed on me a few weeks later when I was invited to give a talk on the Strategic Air Command at a conference of NATO Parliamentarians in Paris, France. After I had presented my prepared—and properly "cleared"—talk, the Parliamentarians, representing the legislative bodies of the fifteen NATO nations, quizzed me at length regarding the effect of the Sputnik launching on SAC's strike capability. Although I could assure them that this had been merely a scientific experiment which had no immediate effect whatever on SAC's role as the Free World's principal military deterrent, I doubt that I managed to allay fully their concern.

A similar attitude was shown in a subsequent press conference, and I repeated my efforts to explain SAC's continued capability to deter aggression not only against the United States but also its allies. This led one of the reporters to ask me whether the SAC B-47s we had in England carried nuclear weapons. It was a tricky question to answer because the fact that these airplanes did carry nuclear weapons was highly classified at that time. Still, I felt very strongly that it would be wrong to protect myself by an outright denial which, sooner or later, would prove to be untrue. Moreover, I considered it imperative to counter the adverse effect of Sputnik with something that I hoped would encourage our allies without actually committing a security violation. Therefore, I replied guardedly: "Well, we did not build these bombers to carry crushed rose petals!"

The effect of this statement was immediate and went beyond what I had intended. Interpreting it correctly, the news media featured it prominently together with excited editorial comments. As could be anticipated, there was angry reaction in the Communist countries, but there was also much criticism in England and attacks on the government which had permitted us to place nuclear weapons on British soil. Nor did I myself escape criticism on the part of my superiors, who felt that my reply had not been diplomatic enough. But the end result of this affair was most salutary. Our enemies had learned that SAC's global alert posture was not an empty threat, and our friends were made to realize that they had to accept the existence of *our* nuclear weapons as their best safeguard against the nuclear weapons of an aggressor.

Since then, there has been a great deal of progress in the public's attitude toward the presence of nuclear weapons—either mounted in missiles which are emplaced near their cities or carried in bombers which fly on airborne alert over their heads. But we still have a long way to go in trying to keep the Communists convinced that our weaknesses are much less critical and our strengths far more significant than theirs. And we continue to impair our deterrent posture by our tendency to play down our military superiority although it is the very foundation of that posture.

Perhaps we are afraid to rock the coexistence boat by appearing too militant and "aggressive" to our enemies. I remember an experience early in 1964 when I went on an inspection trip of military installations in the Far East which was to include Saigon, capital of embattled South Vietnam. I was requested to omit the visit to Saigon as my presence there might be construed by the Communists as an indication that we planned to use SAC bombers against North Vietnam which, of course, was not the case at all.

Perhaps the average American's traditional mistrust of the "man on horseback" and his dislike for all things military in peacetime, fostered by some recent books and motion pictures, are reflected in the desire to avoid all talk and actions that may seem like "saber-rattling" and "warmongering." Or perhaps we are just too anxious to be loved by everybody in this world and to create the image of a peaceable nation that would much prefer to do away with all arms.

But whatever the reasons for this attitude, we must learn to be more realistic if we are sincere in our deterrent role. And we must always remember that the Soviets' decision to initiate a general nuclear war will be guided by two factors—their conviction that they cannot achieve their goals through any other means and their assessment of their military strength vs. ours. This assessment will be based not merely on what they believe to be our strength-in-being. It will be based on the strength they believe we will have left *after* they have subjected us to the massive surprise attack with nuclear bombs and missiles which they are planning.

This brings me to another factor in the deterrent equation, namely, the survivability of our retaliatory strike forces in the face of such an attack. As I will describe in the following chapter, we are employing four basic methods for enhancing the survivability of these forces, and I am convinced that we will retain sufficient striking power, even under the most unfavorable conditions, to counterattack decisively. But, again, it is not enough that *we* are convinced; it is even more important that we keep the Soviets convinced. Hence, in trying to impress on them the credibility of our military superiority, we must also get them to know that this superiority will prevail "under any set of conditions and circumstances."

Finally, even the most credible and survivable military superiority has little deterrent value unless it is backed by the demonstrated determination of the American people to use it, if and as necessary for the protection of our national interests. We demonstrated this determination, to a point, in the Cuban crisis of 1962. We demonstrated it even more convincingly four years earlier when the small republic of Lebanon in the Middle East appealed to the United States for help, following the assassination of King Faisal of neighboring Iraq and the overthrow of his government.

Responding to this appeal, President Eisenhower immediately ordered marines of the U. S. 6th Fleet into Lebanon to "protect American lives, guarantee Lebanon's independence, and to preserve peace in the Middle East." Within barely a day following the Iraq coup, the first battalion of 1,800 marines had occupied the international airport of Lebanon's capital Beirut, a second battalion was ready to land, and reinforcements were being airlifted from the States and Europe in a huge realignment of U. S. military power. Moreover, the entire Strategic Air Command had gone on full alert status for the first time in its history, and all SAC bombers, loaded with nuclear weapons, were poised to strike at a moment's notice.

Despite his threats of intervention and of action against our troops, Khrushchev chose to back down, and the Lebanon crisis was resolved peacefully. What caused Khrushchev to give in was not the presence of our troops, whom he could have over-powered with his far larger forces massed nearby, but the un-mistakable determination of our government to launch the nu-clear might of SAC against the Soviets if they harmed a single American soldier. And it was not only the determination of our government that impressed Khrushchev; there could be no doubt that the majority of the American people supported the resolute action of their government, fully aware of the risks it entailed.

Our determination to make use of our full military superi-ority was also demonstrated with equal success that same year, 1958, when we kept the Red Chinese from seizing Quemoy and other offshore islands under control of the Nationalist Chinese, despite the threat of Soviet intervention. And we demonstrated our determination just as convincingly in helping the freedom-loving people of isolated West Berlin in their valiant struggle against Communist take-over.

All these actions, from Lebanon to Cuba, were good actions, not "irresponsible brinksmanship" as some of our people called it, nor warlike as the Communists claimed, but peaceful because they strengthened the cause of deterrence by following one of its basic principles. Nevertheless, we cannot afford to let these few successes induce us to relax. It is the job of the Soviet hier-archy to keep on testing the determination of the American people and to ascertain how far it can go in its aggressive ven-tures without challenging that determination. A case in point is the erection of the infamous Berlin Wall which proved to the Soviets that they can go quite far indeed without risking any-thing worse than meaningless diplomatic protests.

I believe it is imperative that we do not wait for serious crises to prove our determination to apply the military superiority we possess. We can achieve the same purpose by proving it through our attitude, our expressions and our actions, not only to our enemies but also to our friends. I do not feel that we have been very circumspect and effective in that respect. When President Charles de Gaulle of France announced that he would create his own *"force de frappe"*—nuclear strike force—he was severely criticized by his NATO allies, especially the United States. But I think his primary motive was simply lack of confidence in our determination to come to the aid of France if she should be attacked, and thereby risk nuclear war.

Thus, we owe it to ourselves *and* our allies to let our enemies know that we have incontestable military superiority and that we are determined to use any part or all of it, as may be necessary for the protection of our common security. Moreover, it is not enough to speak in generalities; we must be willing to present facts to lend credibility to our military superiority, our war-winning capability, and our deterrent. Generalities may arouse emotions, but only facts can convince.

These, then, are some of the basic principles which I consider indispensable prerequisites of a successful deterrent posture. To make them abundantly clear, let me summarize them as follows:

1. We must maintain a credible capability to achieve a *military* victory under any set of conditions and circumstances.

   a. To attain this objective, we must possess assured superiority in strategic strike capability.
   b. The superiority of our strategic strike forces must be large enough to be credible and safe enough to prevail even under the most unfavorable condition—a massive nuclear surprise attack.
   c. Our strategic strike forces must be strengthened and modernized continuously, as required to maintain our "deterrent margin."

2. We must make certain that the Soviets and any other potential aggressors know at all times that we have an assured war-winning capability.

a. We must emphasize rather than belittle our strengths if we are to keep our enemies convinced of our military superiority.

b. We must make every effort to impress on the Soviets that we have an unquestionable war-winning capability and that we have taken adequate measures to preserve that capability, even in the face of a massive surprise attack.

c. We must continuously demonstrate to our friends and enemies, through both word and action, that we have the determination to apply our military superiority as may be necessary to protect our interests and those of our allies.

8. The Tools of Deterrence

NEAR the entrance of Offutt Air Force Base, home of the headquarters of the Strategic Air Command, stands a large sign with the SAC emblem and its motto, PEACE IS OUR PROFESSION.

The SAC emblem, a mailed fist offering a choice of olive branch and thunderbolts, aptly illustrates SAC's mission of deterrence. But I have sometimes wondered whether the motto PEACE IS OUR PROFESSION is really fitting for a combat organization that can loose more destructive power than any other military force in history.

Yet, this motto seems well justified because the primary objective of our national policy of deterrence is to maintain peace "under honorable conditions," and none of our military tools of deterrence has contributed more to that objective than the Strategic Air Command. With over 90 percent of the nuclear firepower of the entire Free World carried in its missiles and bombers, SAC still represents the nation's most powerful deterrent tool. Moreover, SAC is the only U. S. military command designed solely for strategic aerospace operations, the very backbone of our posture for deterring aggression and preserving peace.

In discussing the tools of deterrence it is, therefore, appropriate to begin with SAC, not only because it is the foremost tool, but also because its evolution has pointed the way for the evolution of deterrence itself. Still more important, SAC's superior striking power has provided and still does provide an assured war-winning capability which I consider the most essential factor in the effective deterrence of aggression.

Paradoxically enough, the Strategic Air Command is at once the best known and least understood weapon in our arsenal of deterrence. A great deal has been said and written about its vital role in general nuclear war, but much remains to be told of its equally important role in conventional or "limited" wars and of its real significance in deterring war, any kind of war. For SAC is no longer just a tool for "massive retaliation"; always keeping a step ahead of the Soviets in their rapid buildup of their offensive and defensive strength, SAC has developed into a strategic force of unmatched flexibility and versatility.

I have been close to this development almost from the very start because I first joined SAC in 1948, only two years after its establishment, when General Curtis E. LeMay became its Commander and asked me to be his Deputy. During his nine years as Commander, General LeMay transformed SAC from a motley collection of World War II airplanes into a powerful strike force of modern bombers, despite the serious handicap of continuous "peaks and valleys" in military appropriations. I can appreciate the difficulties and magnitude of his achievement perhaps better than anyone else because, as his Vice-Commander during most of that time, I had the privilege of participating in this dramatic transformation.

In 1954 I was appointed Commander of the Air Research and Development Command (later renamed the "Air Force Systems Command") which took me away from SAC for a while. But as it turned out, this proved a most beneficial assignment for me, primarily because I happened to be in command of ARDC when it was given the historic directive to undertake an accelerated program for the development of ballistic missiles. The experiences I gained by being intimately connected with the missile development effort proved invaluable to me when, in 1957, I returned to SAC as Commander in Chief, upon General LeMay's reassignment to Washington, and had to assume the responsibility for the operational employment of this revolutionary new weapon.

With ballistic missiles about to enter both the Soviets' and our strategic inventories, I found SAC facing an unprecedented two-pronged challenge requiring another major transformation. First, we now had to take into account that ICBMs would give the Soviets the capability to destroy SAC strike forces on the ground with little or no warning and thus minimize the threat of retaliation, the very foundation of our deterrent posture. (The only warning system we had at that time was against a bomber attack which would give us several hours to get our bombers off the ground.) Hence, radical changes had to be made in SAC's mode of operations so as to enhance the survivability of its strike forces in the face of a missile attack and thereby preserve our deterrent.

But as the Soviets approached an operational missile capability we were also getting ready to integrate ballistic missiles into our inventory, which resulted in a second task for SAC. This task was to convert SAC from an all-bomber force into a cohesive "mixed force" of bombers and missiles in which one would effectively supplement and complement the other. Both tasks were accomplished in record time, and an entirely new SAC emerged.

Thus the Strategic Air Command has come a long way since it was organized in March 1946. At that time, combat elements of what were then the Army Air Forces were reorganized and regrouped to meet post-World War II conditions. SAC was formed essentially by combining existing medium- and heavy-bomber units, with a total inventory of some 600 aircraft which included 250 propeller-driven bombers. There were only three jet airplanes—holdover F-80 fighters from the war. Total manpower was about 37,000 personnel. Altogether, SAC had 18 active bases.

But small as it was in those early postwar years, SAC was then perhaps a more convincing deterrent than it may ever be again. No other force in the world had atomic bombs; no potential enemy had the capability to prevent SAC from carrying those bombs to his heartlands. Thus any threat of aggression could be easily countered with the threat of devastating retaliation. But as the threat of aggression grew, SAC had to grow with it, both in size and scope.

By the time I retired, in November 1964, SAC's operational inventory included over 2,200 tactical aircraft—most of them all-jet—plus 500 support airplanes as well as more than 800 ICBMs. Manpower had increased to about 260,000—some 35,-000 officers, more than 200,000 airmen and nearly 25,000 civilians. There were 52 SAC bases in the United States and overseas, covering over a million acres, and 18 other locations from which SAC forces operated. The investment in aircraft, missiles, support equipment, inventories and real estate had soared to $21 billion; another $8 billion was invested in the highly specialized training of SAC personnel. SAC's annual operating expense was $2.1 billion, almost $6 million per day or $240,000 per hour.

I am quoting these figures to emphasize two points: first, SAC had to grow considerably in order to keep up with the threat; second, the nation's taxpayers have a huge investment in SAC which not only must be protected but also should be made to yield better dividends through more effective use of SAC as an "all-purpose" deterrent tool.

Nor do statistics alone tell the whole story, impressive as they may be. For SAC is not just airplanes and missiles, bases and real estate, support facilities and personnel. SAC's superior striking power stems from a unique combination of three principal factors: *organization, weapon systems* and *men*. The close coordination and mutual relationship of these factors have brought about a self-sufficient strategic combat system that has the complexity and precision of a fine watch and the span of the globe itself.

It would, therefore, be misleading to compare the strategic capabilities of the United States and the Soviet Union by limiting the comparison to the numbers and performance of equivalent bombers and missiles. To be conclusive, the comparison must be extended to the entire system created for the operation, maintenance and protection of these weapons. Moreover, the quality of the system as a whole depends not only on the quality of each of its components but also on the degree and compatibility of their interrelationship. On the basis of such a comparison, SAC has no counterpart in the world today —and may never have if the proper actions are taken.

To afford a better understanding of *why* SAC is, and can remain, such a superior striking force and deterrent tool, it may be well to take a closer look at what I called the "unique" combination of three principal factors—organization, weapons systems and men.

SAC's *organization* has evolved over the years to serve one purpose only, and that is the effective accomplishment of SAC's global mission "under any set of conditions and circumstances." That mission, briefly stated, is to be continually prepared to destroy *any* aggressor's strategic resources, both military and industrial, to the point where he would no longer have the capacity or will to wage war. SAC has had and still has the capability to accomplish this mission which, as I have emphasized before, is the primary reason why there has been no nuclear war so far. Much of the credit for this success must go to SAC's singular organization, for the planning, support and conduct of its mission required the development of many diverse and highly specialized elements for which there was no precedent in military history.

One of the most vital and largest elements is an unparalleled intelligence system for the collection, storing and utilization of the millions of data which are needed for worldwide target analysis and war planning. This task is so tremendous that it requires the use of the latest electronic computers and a great variety of advanced electronic aids which had to be specially developed. These complex facilities are operated by carefully selected military personnel with many years of intensive training and experience. One of the intelligence sections, which is responsible for calculating the intricate ballistic trajectories for

SAC's missiles, is perhaps the only unit in any combat command that demands advanced degrees in mathematics or related sciences of all its members.

Another vital element in SAC's organization is its worldwide communications network which is doubtless the most advanced and extensive in existence. Representing, in effect, SAC's "nervous system," it assures continuous and instantaneous contact with every SAC component throughout the world and thus permits effective "command and control" of the widely deployed strike forces, an essential factor in maintaining SAC's rapid reaction capability.

SAC's organization further includes a global weather service, worldwide logistics and support systems, facilities for maintaining the proficiency of combat aircraft and missile crews, and many other essential elements. All these elements, individually and in combination, are so flexible that they are readily adaptable to any new condition and requirement.

The focal point of this vast organization is the subterranean Control Center in the headquarters of the Strategic Air Command at Offutt Air Force Base, some ten miles south of Omaha, Nebraska. This Control Center is equipped to present current data on the status of the entire force, to flash instant warning in case of a bomber or missile attack, and to provide all other information and facilities needed by the SAC battle staff to ensure centralized control of the global strike forces.

These strike forces operate a variety of weapon systems—several types of bombers with their associated tankers and several types of missiles. All these weapon systems are integrated into a single cohesive offensive force which is designed to exploit the maximum capabilities of each weapon type for a specific mission objective, yet stresses the effective cooperation and coordination of all combat and support elements toward the joint overall objective. That overall objective can be nothing less than "military victory," as previously defined.

As a force-in-being, SAC must, of course, concentrate its efforts on the accomplishment of its assigned mission on a day-to-day basis. This means that its equipment, although it should always reflect the latest advances in technology, must be well proven and fully operational; that is, reliable and ready for instant use whenever and wherever the need may arise.

The oldest and best proven weapon system in SAC's inventory is the B-47, a rugged and reliable six-jet medium bomber flying at near the speed of sound and at altitudes above 40,000 feet. The "heavyweight" among SAC's current bombers is the eight-jet B-52 Stratofortress, which flies at speeds of over 650 mph and at altitudes above 50,000 feet. Many B-52s are equipped with GAM-77 Hound Dog air-to-ground nuclear-tipped missiles, one carried under each wing, in addition to the normal store of nuclear weapons in their bomb bays. The supersonic and accurately guided Hound Dog can be used by the bomber either to destroy the air defenses ahead or to attack additional targets far off its path. The latest version of the B-52, the B-52H, became operational in 1961 and costs fully equipped, with two Hound Dogs and two decoy missiles for penetration, over $12 million.

Latest of SAC's bombers is the B-58 Hustler, which can fly at more than 1,300 mph—about twice the speed of sound—at altitudes above 60,000 feet. The Free World's only supersonic bomber, the B-58 has set a number of spectacular speed records and thus demonstrated its capability to reach any target on earth in a few hours. The first B-58s were delivered to SAC in 1960.

Although all SAC bombers are designed primarily to deliver nuclear weapons, they can also carry conventional bombs or any other stores, a fact which is not always well understood. The speed, range and carrying capacity of SAC's bombers thus make them also highly effective tools for fighting—and deterring—limited conventional wars.

The unrefueled ranges of these bombers, varying from over 3,000 miles for the B-47 to more than 12,000 miles for the B-52H, can be extended through aerial refueling to virtually any range, limited only by the endurance of the crew. Latest addition to SAC's fleet of "flying filling stations" is the KC-135 four-jet Stratotanker which became operational in 1957 and makes it possible to refuel the jet bombers at their normal speed and altitude, thus saving precious time. Aerial refueling has become a routine operation for SAC's air crews and is carried out day and night, and in any kind of weather.

Thus the bomber component of SAC's mixed force appears to have all the punch and versatility it needs to accomplish its share of the strategic mission. But while this was still true in 1964, the outlook for the future was not at all bright at the time of my retirement, in November. The B-47s were being phased out of the inventory and retired, with no replacement planned. The B-52 production line had long since been shut down. The earlier B-52 models were becoming obsolescent and beginning to show the strain of low-altitude training, necessitated by diversification in SAC's penetration tactics. Only two B-58 wings of 40 aircraft each were in SAC's inventory, and no additional wings had been authorized despite my urgent recommendation to do so.

Above all, plans for eventually replacing any of these bomber types with more advanced aircraft were hazy and pursued without any urgency ever since the controversial B-70 program had been scrapped. (The two models of the B-70 still under development are not intended to be weapon systems but merely "test beds" with no direct operational significance.) The disregard of our future bomber requirements has serious implications, as will be discussed later.

The outlook is considerably brighter for SAC's missile force. This is most gratifying but, at the same time, indicative of the shift in emphasis from the flexible mixed-force concept to a rigid deterrent force consisting primarily or entirely of missiles.

SAC's first Intercontinental Ballistic Missile was the Atlas which became operational in September 1959 when an all-SAC crew successfully launched one of these 75-foot missiles from Vandenberg Air Force Base in California. The more advanced Titan was declared operational less than three years later, in April 1962. And the Minuteman, now SAC's principal ICBM, achieved operational status but eight months later, in December 1962.

Thus, within the short span of only a little over three years, SAC progressed from the first generation of ballistic missiles to ICBMs with far superior features with respect to performance, reaction capability, survivability, cost and manpower requirements. The question may be asked why we went ahead with the production of the original Atlas, through the "F" model, when we knew that within just a few years we would have more advanced, survivable and reliable missiles in the inventory. There are several compelling reasons for that.

In the first place, the Atlas permitted us to start building up our missile force at a time when the Soviets reportedly were doing the same. By avoiding a "missile gap," we prevented the Soviets from gaining a decisive lead in the missile race and thereby maintained the credibility of our deterrent throughout a very crucial period.

Equally important was the fact that the ICBM was a revolutionary new weapon for whose operational employment there was no precedent anywhere. From the day in July 1954 when, as Commander of ARDC, I received the directive to undertake an intensive program for ICBM development, to the first operational launch of an Atlas, only some five years had passed. I consider this a fantastic accomplishment on the part of the nation's civilian and military scientists and engineers. Everything, from the missile itself to the extensive launch facilities and support equipment, had to be created from scratch. It was the early Atlas which made it possible for us to test and improve these facilities as well as develop the organization and skills we would need for the operation and maintenance of the more advanced missiles. Thus we were ready for these missiles when they began to enter SAC's rapidly growing inventory. Another invaluable contribution in this respect was the experience and on-the-job training in missile operations which SAC's new missilemen gained during the difficult transition period from an all-bomber to a mixed force.

It must also be realized that continuous improvements are necessary for any new weapon system, especially if it is as dramatically different from any previous and proven weapon system as the ICBM. These improvements come not only through new discoveries and advances in the state of the art but also through experience in actual operation and through the expanded requirements that result both from such operation and the growth of the "threat."

The first Atlas missiles were "soft," that is, they were kept aboveground with no or little protection and, therefore, were vulnerable to the effects of an enemy missile impacting some distance away. Their guidance system did not permit their launching in salvos. Being, in effect, still in the development stage, their operational reliability was not too good. Their reaction capability was relatively slow because they used liquid, non-storable fuels. This meant that they had to be fueled immediately before launch, with liquid oxygen being "topped off" until just before actual firing.

In the meantime, however, the quantity and accuracy of Soviet missiles had increased to such a degree that "soft" and slow-reacting missiles no longer represented an adequate deterrent. But our missile technology had made much progress also. We developed fuels which can be stored in the missile almost indefinitely, thus greatly decreasing reaction time for launching. Particularly significant in this respect was the development of solid fuels which, in addition to their virtually unlimited storability, permitted much simplification in the missile power plant, leading to a smaller and more reliable ICBM. New launching techniques make it possible to "harden" our missiles by keeping them in well-protected underground silos from which they can be launched directly. Improvements in guidance systems now allow for simultaneous firing of an entire squadron of missiles. Advances in the "packaging" of nuclear power, made before the test ban treaty went into effect, have resulted in smaller missile warheads with greater yields.

These and other advances are incorporated in the Titan II, which uses a storable liquid fuel, and the solid-fueled Minuteman, which has a reaction capability of only 30 seconds. Standing on alert in deep and thickly cemented underground silos, ready for instant firing, these missiles can withstand even a near miss of an enemy missile. It is, however, still a matter of conjecture whether their operability will be affected in any way by certain effects other than blast and heat that may be created by a high-yield nuclear explosion at some distance from the silos. Nor have these missiles ever been tested completely from launch to detonation of the warhead or, without warhead, been launched from an operational site, as authority to do so has always been denied. But launches made from test and training sites, with dummy warheads, have indicated good reliability and extremely high accuracy.

The Minuteman, SAC's latest and principal ICBM, has the added advantage of requiring very few personnel for operation and maintenance because of the greater simplicity of its solid-fuel power plant and associated equipment. Moreover, it is as reliable as anything man can devise and build. At this writing, a total Minuteman force of about 1,000 missiles is programmed, at a cost of some $200 million per squadron of 50 missiles. (This amount includes not only the price of the missiles but also of the complete installation, technical facilities, support and check-out equipment, spares, etc.) As the Minuteman missiles are coming in, the older and more vulnerable Atlas and Titan I missiles are being phased out.

One of the most gratifying aspects of SAC's rapid and successful integration of missiles is the demonstration that the Command is flexible enough to adapt itself to any new weapon system, no matter how revolutionary. This is due, to a large measure, to the unusual type and quality of SAC's personnel—the third factor in SAC's "unique" combination.

To get into and *stay* in SAC, even the average officer and airman must possess far above average qualifications, training and skills. This is mandatory not only because of the unprecedented demands of SAC's global mission but also because of the complexity of its weapon systems and the extensive use of computers and other highly specialized electronic equipment in SAC's communications, intelligence, planning, supply and other support activities. But no greater mental, physical and moral demands are made of military men anywhere than are placed on the men who make up SAC's combat crews.

There are nearly 15,000 men in the bomber and tanker crews and over 4,000 in the missile crews, for a total of approximately 19,000 men or less than 7½ percent of SAC's personnel. These men represent the "cutting edge" of the Strategic Air Command. They are charged with awesome responsibilities which require both the highest degree of professionalism and unlimited dedication to their mission. With a large percentage of SAC's strike forces on alert around the clock, these men must remain at their duty stations for days on end, always ready at a moment's notice to do their difficult job, either in one of the frequent tests or—in earnest. No general or admiral in all of history ever had as much firepower under his control as has a single bomber or missile crew with its nuclear weapons today. Therefore, the utmost care in the selection of these crews was one of the primary measures SAC had to take in order to make the accidental or inadvertent firing of a nuclear weapon all but impossible.

To maintain at least half of SAC's entire bomber-tanker force on alert at all times, in the continental United States as well as at the overseas bases, crewmen must work an average of 74 hours a week (*including* leave and other time off) and spend some 135 days a year on alert duty, away from their homes and families. And they are by no means all youngsters, because it takes many years and, in the case of a B-52 commander, as much as $1.2 million to get them ready to assume command positions in the war plan. Commanders of "senior" and "select" aircraft crews average thirty-seven years of age; many of them are combat veterans, and they have an average of over a dozen years of flying experience.

I have often been asked what makes men with such superior qualities choose to stay in SAC—and most of them do—instead of accepting tempting offers from commercial air lines and industry, which would mean not only much better pay but also a far less rigorous job and a more stable and pleasant life. It may seem trite to say that they are motivated to remain in the Service and in SAC by patriotism, dedication and belief in the vital importance of their mission. Yet there is usually no other explanation, just as it is difficult to explain what makes a missionary follow his calling in the steaming jungle or a fireman risk his life to save a child in a burning house.

I think this nation is fortunate indeed to have enough men who are both qualified and willing to remain on SAC combat crews because, without them, we could never maintain a convincing deterrent. The least the American people should do for them is to make certain that they receive equitable monetary compensation for the sacrifices they and their families have to make. Incredibly, the opposite is true. More and more of the traditional military privileges which have been an integral part of military compensation—commissaries, exchanges, etc.—are being curtailed because of the objections of a few local merchants. Nor have the infrequent raises that have been granted kept step with soaring living expenses and pay increases in civilian life.

I do not propose to pay, for example, a SAC B-52 commander the $30,000-plus earned by the captain of a luxurious commercial jetliner—although he would be worth every penny of it—because what SAC needs is not for sale. However, he and all other professional military personnel should earn at least enough to provide a fair living for themselves and their families. Too, there should be some way of giving extra compensation to those who must perform the grueling alert duty, even if it is just enough to serve as a token of appreciation. I have tried for years to obtain a small amount of alert pay for SAC's combat crews but all I was able to get were expressions of sympathetic regret.

I submit that all this is very shortsighted policy, and I am bringing up the matter of military compensation at this point because it has a direct bearing on our ability to preserve an adequate deterrent throughout the future. It took many years to get together the nucleus of professionals who are the core of SAC's fighting strength. If we should lose these men and discourage younger ones from getting ready to take their places, we would not only lose the billions of dollars invested in their training but would also destroy an incomparable combat organization which we may never have the time or opportunity to build up again should the need arise. The harmful effects of outmoded personnel policies can be exceeded only, in this and many other respects, by the potentially disastrous consequences of those policies which advisedly strive for the gradual elimination of our manned strategic forces.

SAC's organization, weapon systems and personnel combine to assure superior striking capability *today*. But problems exist which gravely impair the preservation of SAC's superiority and war-winning capability for the critical years ahead. Some of these problems can be resolved only by an enlightened and aroused public, through their elected representatives. But there are also other problems of an essentially military nature which SAC has been able or is trying to resolve by itself although, here again, it needs public understanding and support. Foremost among these problems is the survivability of SAC's strike forces in the face of a massive surprise attack.

As I indicated before, it is very unlikely that the Soviets would undertake a deliberate attack on the United States unless they were confident that they could keep the damage to be expected from our retaliatory attack within "acceptable limits." This means that they must either develop effective defenses against all our offensive weapon systems and strategies—an all but impossible task as long as we have a mixed force—or must destroy the bulk of our strategic strike forces *before* they can be launched. The Soviets could conceivably achieve the latter objective through a well-planned surprise attack, and once they are convinced that they can do so successfully, the danger of nuclear aggression would become very real and imminent. Hence, the survivability of our retaliatory forces, as assessed by the Soviets or any other potential aggressor, is one of the prime factors in maintaining a credible deterrent.

The complex problems of survivability with which we have

to cope today are relatively new because, until a few years ago, the main threat our strike forces faced was a Soviet bomber attack. To help meet this threat was the task of the North American Air Defense Command or NORAD, a joint U. S.-Canadian organization with headquarters in Colorado Springs, Colorado. NORAD is composed of the U. S. Air Force's Air Defense Command; the U. S. Army's Air Defense Command; the U. S. Naval Forces, NORAD; and the Royal Canadian Air Force's Air Defense Command. A dual mission was assigned to NORAD—to provide warning of a Soviet bomber attack and to accomplish the four basic functions of air defense: detection, identification, interception and destruction of enemy bombers.

NORAD's principal "customer" for warning was—and still is—SAC. Direct liaison and a closed-circuit TV system were established between the two headquarters to provide the key staff in SAC's Control Center with continuous and instant information on the air situation. In this manner, NORAD's vast network of radar stations, stretching across the roof of the continent down to the southern border of the United States, could give SAC sufficient warning of a bomber attack to get a sizable part of its bomber-tanker forces airborne before they could be destroyed on the ground. Moreover, NORAD's well-coordinated team of anti-aircraft defenses and interceptors could be expected to give attacking enemy bombers a good fight.

But the situation changed dramatically when the Soviets achieved an operational ballistic-missile capability. While we must still maintain warning and defenses against their bombers, this threat has become secondary to that posed by their missiles. There is as yet no defense against ballistic missiles, and because of their tremendous speed—taking them from launch in Russia to impact in the United States in about half an hour—warning has been compressed to just a few minutes.

Warning of a missile attack is provided by NORAD's new Ballistic Missile Early Warning System (BMEWS) which consists of three huge radar installations located at Clear, Alaska; Thule, Greenland; and Flyingdales Moor in England. The powerful radar beams of the three BMEWS stations, fanning out and overlapping, probe thousands of miles into the sky and toward the Soviet Union. If any objects cross the beam fans, fantastically complex computers rapidly analyze this event and determine whether these objects are missiles or perhaps just meteorites. Should the computers conclude that a missile attack is in progress, they flash this information—together with the number of missiles involved, their origin, and anticipated time and location of impact—to the NORAD Combat Operations Center. From there, all information is relayed instantly to the Command Post at SAC Headquarters, and to the Air Force Command Post and Joint War Room in the Pentagon.

Since the BMEWS radars spot enemy missiles near their apogee—the highest point in their ballistic trajectory—they can provide, at best, some fifteen minutes' warning. Too, such warning is presently limited to missiles coming in from the north. Should the Soviets succeed in developing missiles which, without degradation in accuracy, can be fired the long way around the South Pole, we would have no warning against them. This would also be true for missiles launched from Soviet submarines within a few hundred miles off our coasts. (The ballistic missiles which the Soviets tried to place on Cuba could have hit us with virtually no warning which was the main reason why we had to get those missiles taken out, one way or another.)

Because of the vital importance of timely warning to the preservation of our deterrent, I have repeatedly and urgently recommended an all-out effort for the development of an omnidirectional warning system and, subsequently, of satellites capable of detecting the firing of missiles within a few seconds after launch. Unfortunately, little progress has been made in this respect.

In view of these and related problems SAC is employing four different principles to enhance the survivability of its strike forces. The first principle is based on fast reaction coupled with warning and applies only to the manned forces. Knowing the optimum amount of warning SAC can expect to get of a missile attack—some fifteen minutes, at least for the time being—the largest possible percentage of the manned forces is postured in such a way that it can be airborne within less than that time and, thereby, escape destruction on the ground. And that is the principle behind SAC's ground alert system.

Beginning in the fall of 1957 with a small percentage of the force, the alert was gradually expanded until now about half of the entire bomber-tanker force is maintained on continuous alert status. The airplanes are fueled and cocked to go. The alert crews on duty live and sleep nearby, spending much of their time checking and rechecking their assigned targets and their routes, studying the latest weather data. Practice alerts at any time of day or night make them race to their aircraft, never knowing whether this is only a test or the "real thing." In this manner, every action and movement become routine with them, and they are fully prepared to get airborne in less than the fifteen minutes of BMEWS warning.

Never before in military history has it been attempted to keep such a high percentage of a large combat force on constant alert during peacetime, let alone to do so month after month, year after year. To achieve this—and to achieve it at minimum risk and cost—SAC had to make radical changes and innovations in traditional military management, procedures and safeguards. Perhaps the most important of the special procedures developed for the alert is the Positive Control system which, under the name "Fail Safe," has been given much erroneous and misleading publicity. Here is how the system really works:

If warning of an attack is received from NORAD, the SAC Commander in Chief is authorized to launch the ground alert force. He does not have the authority to send the force to war—this authority rests entirely with the President of the United States—but he can and would launch the alert force for one purpose only, and that is to prevent its threatened destruction on the ground.

Once in the air, the bombers fly toward a designated point on their routes which is well outside enemy radars. After reaching that point, the bombers return to their bases *unless* they receive coded voice instructions to proceed to their targets. The "go code" can be given only upon direct orders of the President, and it must be authenticated by officers at each of several levels of command and by more than one member of the bomber crew. Coordinated action by several crew members is also required to arm nuclear weapons after the "go code" has been received and authenticated.

The "go-code" is transmitted to the airborne force by a variety of means and from widely separted transmitters in order to ensure its receipt. But if, for some unlikely reason, a bomber should not receive the attack order or if there is any doubt whatever regarding proper authentication, that bomber would turn back after reaching the "Positive Control" point and "Fail Safe." Thus, the worst thing that could happen would be to leave, in case of an actual enemy attack, one or more targets in the aggressor's territory uncovered, a risk that must be accepted in order to guarantee against inadvertent action. And if the warning should prove spurious, the launch of the alert force would amount to nothing more than a training exercise. (To protect against any possible ruse on the part of an aggressor, a back-up force is readied immediately upon launch of the alert force.)

One question I have been asked quite frequently pertains to the possibility that if there should be an actual attack, the President might not be able to give the order to counterattack, either because he may not be immediately available or may have become incapacitated. This problem has long been recognized and adequate provisions have been taken to make certain that there will always be someone with proper authority to give the necessary order. Also, the Positive Control system gives our civil authorities several hours to reach a decision as the bombers need not receive the order to proceed until they have reached the Positive Control point on their route.

I never had to launch the alert force in earnest during all my years as Commander in Chief of SAC, although I was close to doing so several times. Shortly after the BMEWS became operational, I received the alarming message one night that the BMEWS board in SAC's Command Post indicated a number of high-flying objects being headed toward the United States. My first impulse was to launch the ground-alert force as a precautionary measure but, after quick consultation with my controllers and the controllers at NORAD, we decided that the BMEWS system was still too unproven to warrant action in response to signals which, to all indications, had to be caused by something other than enemy missiles. As we found out later, the signals had been caused by BMEWS radar beams bouncing off the moon and, needless to say, steps were taken at once to eliminate our natural satellite as a potential source of false alarm.

Another time—again, as usual, in the middle of the night—the SAC controller on duty advised me tersely that all communications with the BMEWS sites and NORAD had been suddenly disrupted. There could be only one of two reasons for that—enemy action or a communications failure. As I could not take any chances, I ordered the alert crews to their airplanes, ready for takeoff, which was nothing unusual for the crews even at that time of night. While they were racing to their aircraft, I had about two or three minutes to decide whether I should actually launch the force. I used this brief time to establish contact with a SAC plane flying over the Thule site and learned that nothing untoward had happened. Thereupon I had the crews returned to their alert shacks and, as far as they were concerned, this had been just another practice alert. Shortly after, normal communications with the BMEWS sites and NORAD were restored, and action was taken immediately to correct what turned out to be a minor deficiency in the communications link.

Since then, continuous improvements have made the BMEWS a very reliable and dependable missile warning system. At the same time, SAC continued its efforts to shave precious seconds from the reaction time of its alert forces. One important achievement in this respect was the introduction of the "Minimum Interval Takeoff" (MITO) procedure. In the past, SAC's airplanes could not take off in less than one-minute intervals because of the dense clouds of smoke trailed by each airplane as it spurted down the runway. This meant that, if there were for instance ten bombers on alert at a particular base, their takeoff alone would consume some ten minutes which I considered dangerously long in case of a surprise attack. Therefore, I initiated tests which proved that, by resort-ing to some novel techniques, we could reduce the interval to fifteen seconds, thus cutting total takeoff time to one-fourth of what it had been. I would not recommend that procedure for routine operations because it takes the superior skill and expe-rience of SAC crews to make it safe.

SAC's reaction capability was demonstrated dramatically to the late President Kennedy when he visited a base where eight B-52s were kept on alert. He and his party were seated with me near the runway, in sight of the parked aircraft. The crews were in the alert shack nearby, pursuing their normal activities. Then the President gave me the signal, and I relayed his order to the SAC Command Post. Within seconds the alert crews sprinted out of their building, and the last B-52 was airborne only some seven minutes after the President had signaled me.

Perhaps the most striking feature of this demonstration was the fact that it was a routine operation which could be ex-pected to be just as rapid and precise in response to a real alert. This has been proven in several non-routine operations where SAC could demonstrate its reaction capability as well as its ver-satility. One such operation was SAC's participation in the Cu-ban crisis, described earlier. Another operation took place in March 1964 when SAC B-52 and B-58 bombers, equipped with special cameras, were airborne within two hours' notice and en route to provide extensive photographic coverage of the Alas-kan earthquake damage.

In addition to its rapid reaction capability, SAC resorts to the principle of dispersal to enhance the survivability of its strike forces, both manned and unmanned. Wide dispersal not only increases an aggressor's target system but also minimizes the effect of each hit.

Normal dispersal of the manned force can be greatly ex-panded in an emergency as was done during the Cuban crisis when small B-47 units were deployed to a considerable number of non-SAC bases and civilian airfields. SAC bombers are also dispersed to overseas bases in an operation called "Reflex." Rotating on a regular schedule, Reflex crews take their aircraft to specified overseas bases for certain periods of time during which they remain on alert. For political and economic reasons the number of SAC's overseas bases has been greatly reduced. This reduction has not affected SAC's strike capability to any marked degree. However, considering the military advantages of global dispersal of our strategic strike forces and its benefits to the Free World's overall deterrent, it should be worthwhile to retain at least some of the key foreign bases for SAC.

SAC's ICBMs are dispersed countrywide by squadron and, within each squadron, in such a manner that individual missiles are at least "one bomb apart," that is, spaced far enough from each other so that one enemy bomb or missile cannot destroy more than one of our missiles at a time. To further aggravate an aggressor's problem, SAC is using a third principle for lessening the vulnerability of its ICBMs, namely, "hardening."

"Hardening" is the term used generally for physical protection, such as the deep underground silos with thick concrete walls in which SAC's latest missiles are kept on alert. Hardening would not be practical for aircraft although it can and is being used for the protection of fuel and weapons storage and, in a broader sense, of communications. "Hardening," as applied to communications, refers not only to physical protection of equipment and cabling but, even more so, to redundancy or back-up so that, if one circuit or system is destroyed, other circuits and systems are available to take over.

The combination of dispersal and hardening is a most important strategy for the protection of SAC's missiles. Although over 90 per cent of these missiles are on alert at all times, they cannot be launched upon receipt of warning as can the manned alert force for its protection. If the warning should prove spurious, missiles once launched cannot be recalled and they must, therefore, "ride out" the initial attack which calls for the most convincing protective measures possible. The combination of dispersal and hardening is particularly effective in this respect because it places almost impossible demands on an aggressor with respect to the numbers and accuracy of his missiles as well as the simultaneity of their impact.

While nothing man has built so far—or may ever build—can withstand a direct hit of a hydrogen bomb, the destructive power of a nuclear explosion decreases rapidly with distance. Therefore, accuracy becomes more decisive than nuclear yield in trying to destroy a small and very hard target such as a missile silo. But accuracy varies from missile to missile, and several missiles must be programmed against each target in order to be reasonably confident that one of them will score a direct hit on that target.

Knowing the average accuracy of their missiles as well as their operational reliability and nuclear yield, the Soviet war planners can figure out the number of missiles they would have to program against one of ours in order to have the desired degree of confidence—say, 90 percent—that it will be destroyed. While this number would decrease greatly as the Soviets improve their missile accuracy and reliability, they still would have to target several missiles against each of ours if they want to be sufficiently confident that they can destroy all or most of our hardened and dispersed missiles.

Moreover, all Soviet missiles would have to be launched from their widely scattered sites throughout Russia in such a manner as to hit all of our equally scattered missiles almost simultaneously. If they would fail to do so, less than one minute's delay in impacts would provide sufficient warning to launch our surviving Minuteman missiles.

Thus, wide dispersal and hardening of our fast-reacting missiles greatly add to the credibility of our deterrent. But we cannot preserve the deterrent value of these missiles for any length of time as long as there is an arbitrary limit for the maximum number to be procured, as is presently the case. As the Soviets keep increasing the number, accuracy and reliability of *their* missiles, we must increase the number of *our* land-based missiles commensurately if we are to prevent the Soviets from ever reaching the point where they would feel confident that they can destroy the bulk of SAC's missile force in a surprise attack. For this reason, we must maintain the capability to produce additional and, preferably, still more advanced ICBMs, as may be required by future conditions and changes in the threat.

A fourth and highly effective strategy for improving survivability is *mobility*. The principle behind this strategy is to keep the entire weapon system moving at all times so that an aggressor's war planners cannot predict where it will be located at the precise time of the attack which they are planning and, therefore, cannot target a missile against it. Mobility is the principle of survivability employed by the Polaris submarine and SAC's airborne alert.

The same principle was to be used for a mobile Minuteman system in which a number of regular Minuteman missiles were to be mounted on railroad cars and moved in a random pattern over the almost 100,000 miles of railroad trackage in this country that is suitable for this purpose. Each of the 60 Minuteman trains proposed was to be entirely self-sufficient and included, in addition to five missiles in fast-erecting launchers, all necessary communications, electronic and power equipment as well as living quarters for the crew. Beginning in 1960, an experimental Minuteman train was tested extensively and with complete success. However, the Department of Defense suddenly cancelled the program in December 1961, and my repeated efforts to have it reinstated were to no avail. I still feel very strongly that a mobile Minuteman system, either on railroad cars or trucks, is not only feasible and economically justified but, because of its excellent survivability, would also add immeasurably to the nation's arsenal of deterrence. For this reason I hope that the program will be resumed and completed at the earliest possible time.

I had similar problems with the airborne alert although my efforts were somewhat more successful. As its name implies, the airborne alert is an operation in which a certain percentage of SAC's bombers is kept in the air continuously and in an alert condition, that is, ready to proceed to their targets whenever they should receive the "go code." Being far beyond any enemy's reach and countermeasures, bombers on airborne alert are virtually invulnerable, even in case of a massive surprise attack without any warning at all.

I first suggested the airborne alert in the late 1950s when it became apparent that the Soviets were building up a sizable inventory of ballistic missiles. We still did not have any warning against a missile attack at that time, and I felt that an airborne alert could ensure the survival of enough heavy bombers, even under the worst condition, to maintain an impressive retaliatory capability. However, my superiors in Washington did not share my beliefs and insisted that an airborne alert would not be practical because of wear and tear on the aircraft, excessive fuel consumption, logistic problems and other reasons. Nevertheless, SAC was permitted to develop and test airborne alert techniques, on a small scale and out of its own resources, and these tests proved convincingly that a sustained airborne alert was both feasible and practical.

In January 1960 I gave a prepared talk in New York in which I was allowed to say that, if the Soviets had 150 ICBMS and another 150 IRBMs, they would have a 95 percent probability of wiping out our entire nuclear strike capability, as it then existed, within a span of 30 minutes. I added that an airborne alert offered at least a partial solution to the problem posed by such a threat, if and when it should materialize. My statements created considerable discussion and controversy, and the then Secretary of Defense, Thomas S. Gates, told me later that this matter had caused him more trouble than anything else he had encountered during his tenure of office.

A few weeks after my New York talk I was required to substantiate the claims I had made at a joint hearing of the Senate Committee on Aeronautical and Space Sciences and the Preparedness Subcommittee of the Senate Committee on Armed Services. (The chairman of both the committee and the subcommittee happened to be the then Senator Lyndon B. Johnson.) After detailed testimony, I received wholehearted support for the airborne-alert concept. This proved instrumental in bringing about action by other committees which gave the Department of Defense virtually a blank check for creating an extensive airborne-alert capability to be used in emergencies—an unprecedented action indeed. Thereupon the Department of Defense authorized SAC to initiate a limited but regular schedule of airborne alert missions for training purposes and to establish an "on-the-shelf" capability for expanding this schedule so as to place a substantial percentage of the B-52 fleet on sustained airborne alert, whenever the need to do so should arise.

This capability proved most useful during the Cuban crisis when Cuba-based Soviet missiles could have hit our ground-alert forces without warning. It is likely that we may need this capability again, and perhaps on a larger scale than presently provided for, if we are threatened with a missile attack from a direction or source against which we have no reliable warning.

One type of airborne alert that has been flown continuously since early 1961 is SAC's Airborne Command Post, known as "Looking Glass." The purpose of this operation is to ensure continuity of one of SAC's most important management functions—command and control of the global strike forces.

Command and control are normally exercised from the underground command post at SAC Headquarters. Provisions have been made for alternate command posts throughout the United States to take over automatically if the SAC command post should be destroyed in an attack. But when the danger arose that all command posts might be hit at the same or nearly the same time, means had to be found to provide an invulnerable back-up, and that means proved to be an *airborne* command post.

SAC now maintains in the air at all times a modified KC-135 Jet Stratotanker which is equipped with all the communications gear and special staff required to serve as an emergency command post. There is always a general officer aboard who is qualified to assume command of the SAC force and to direct execution of the "Emergency War Order" in the event all command posts on the ground have been lost. Several KC-135s are held in readiness for these missions, and not a single mission has ever been canceled, aborted or met with an accident since the operation was started years ago.

Thus, using all four survivability strategies—fast reaction coupled with warning, dispersal, hardening, and mobility—SAC can be certain that a sufficient percentage of its strike forces, as well as their command and control, will survive under any circumstances to retain superior strike capability. But, again, this is true *today*, and whether this will be true five or ten years hence will depend entirely on the timely and necessary actions taken to meet future threats.

While SAC has been able so far to cope with the problem of survivability of its strike forces in the face of *external* aggression, it has no way of dealing with a survivability problem that stems from *internal* causes. I am referring to the growing trend in this country to shift from the concept of deterrence through superior striking power, as represented by SAC, to the principle of defensive deterrence, as advocated by those who propose just enough retaliatory capability to maintain a stalemate.

The increasing belief that a credible war-winning capability is no longer feasible and that a limited number of ballistic missiles on land and at sea would suffice to make nuclear war "impossible" may lead to decisions which could seriously impair the preservation of SAC's superior striking power. I am particularly concerned about the maintenance of a well-balanced mixed force because it is this type of force which, in my opinion, has been the key to the nation's assured capability to win and, therefore, deter any kind of war.

For this reason I feel very strongly that all necessary actions should be taken without delay to provide SAC with the quantity and quality of advanced manned systems which it will need in the future to maintain a balanced and effective mixed force. Unless such actions are taken, I am afraid that the dawning space age may find SAC shrunk to a purely defensive missile command, with a few obsolete and battered bombers. Such a

SAC would have little if any deterrent value once new threats loom from space and Communist China has built up its nuclear capability to the point where it could undertake nuclear aggression against its neighbors, if not the United States.

I may be accused of being prejudiced in favor of bombers because of my long association with SAC which, until not so long ago, was strictly a bomber force. But the truth of the matter is that I chose to spend almost half of my military career, up to my statutory retirement, in SAC because I always have had and still have implicit faith in its mission. And both the facts and my experiences convinced me that this mission can now and in the future be accomplished only with a balanced mixed force of manned and unmanned strategic weapon systems.

I have been closely connected with ballistic missiles, from the early development stage of the first generation to its phase-out from the operational inventory and the phase-in of the next generation. This experience has permitted me to arrive at a realistic appraisal of the unique advantages of ballistic missiles but also of their limitations.

By the same token, I have been actively engaged in bomber operations for over three decades and thus became thoroughly familiar with the unique advantages and limitations of manned weapon systems. In directing the development of SAC's mixed-force concept I endeavored to exploit the advantages of both types of weapon systems to the fullest so that they could effectively complement and supplement one another. Following this precept, SAC achieved invaluable flexibility in its operations, affording a wide choice of weapon systems and tactics in selecting the most suitable ones for each type of strategic mission. At the same time, the numerous combinations of different weapon systems and tactics which SAC can employ pose a many-sided technological and military problem for the Soviets, forcing them to scatter their defense efforts and seriously draining their already strained economy.

The principal feature which the ballistic missile contributes to SAC's mixed-force operation is its tremendous speed—some 15,000 miles per hour. Coupled with the rapid reaction capability of the latest missiles, this speed permits almost instant response to aggression and effective attacks on "time-sensitive" targets, that is, Soviet missile sites and bomber fields from which early follow-on strikes could be launched. Carrying a nuclear warhead, the ballistic missile is the most potent weapon ever devised against "area" targets, such as cities and industrial complexes or large military installations. And since missile accuracy has improved greatly, attacks on smaller and "hard" targets have also become feasible.

There is as yet no defense against ballistic missiles, and countermeasures already are under development to deal with any anti-missile defenses that can be anticipated. Increasing automation has greatly reduced the manning requirements for missile sites and, being unmanned themselves, missiles entail no risks to air crews as do bombers.

The point has been made that ballistic missiles are particularly attractive weapons for an aggressor who plans a massive surprise attack in order to achieve a decisive and none-too-costly victory. Conversely, these missiles are considered very suitable for deterrence of aggression if they are used as "threat weapons" against urban and industrial centers. While these rather general statements may be true, the more advanced ballistic missiles also lend themselves very well to a variety of specialized strategic missions. Increasingly targeted in lieu or in support of bombers, ICBMs now play a vital role in our strategic war planning and have added tremendously to SAC's overall striking power and reaction capability.

The manned bomber lacks some of the missile's advantages but, in turn, has others which are not shared by the missile. Because of the frequently expressed doubts in the future utility of manned strategic weapon systems, it may be well to discuss some of these advantages.

Immediately upon receipt of warning, the ground-alert force can be launched under "Positive Control" and thus becomes practically invulnerable to the effects of an enemy attack. Missiles must "ride out" such an attack as they cannot be recalled if the warning should prove spurious while the manned alert force would turn back automatically in such a case.

Only manned weapon systems can be used for targets whose location is not known accurately enough to direct missiles against them and for targets which are non-stationary or so compact and hard that they require precision bombing.

Bombers can carry the largest nuclear weapons in our inventory, which are too bulky and heavy for missiles, as well as a number of weapons of different yield, permitting them to attack several targets during the same mission. Equipped with Hound Dog air-to-surface missiles, a bomber can in addition hit targets far off its route.

Bombing accuracies are actually measured in feet. Using small nuclear weapons or conventional bombs, the manned bomber can hit a target with the utmost discrimination, destroying not more and not less than the mission calls for.

Being able to carry any type and combination of payload—nuclear weapons, conventional bombs, special-purpose stores, or just photographic equipment—the versatile manned bomber is as useful in the cold war and in non-nuclear conflicts as it is in nuclear war. Its value in non-military emergencies was illustrated by the previously mentioned use of SAC bombers in providing rapid photographic coverage of the wide-spread damage in the Alaskan earthquake.

SAC's long-range bombers become unlimited-range bombers through aerial refueling, placing them in range of any target on earth from their home bases. Routine aerial refueling permits SAC bombers to remain on airborne alert for 24 hours or more; they can circle—and have in fact circled—the globe without landing.

While the ballistic missile's trajectory is fixed and predictable once it is launched, the manned weapon system can make any desired or necessary changes in its flight plan while in route, including changes in targets or mission as may be required by unpredictable circumstances. The versatility and flexibility of the manned bomber make it possible to accomplish missions far too complex for unmanned weapon systems. (This was demonstrated strikingly by SAC exercise "Order Blank" in April 1964. Eight B-52 and B-58 bombers, taking off from widely separated bases, simulated simultaneous "attacks" on six targets in Europe, Africa and Asia, with ranges up to almost 10,-000 miles. Their weapons were—cameras. With permission of the countries concerned, the bombers reached their distant targets within three minutes of each other and scored accurate photographic "hits.")

The flexibility of the manned bomber allows for drastic changes in tactics so as to complicate the enemy's defense problem. SAC bombers were designed to bomb from high altitudes which caused the Soviets to build a multibillion-dollar defense system employing very advanced antiaircraft missiles. But now SAC bombers can operate at any altitude from very high to very low, switching tactics as may be required to deal with the defenses they encounter.

There will always be need for man over enemy territory because no missile computer can match the reasoning power of the human mind. It is that uncanny capacity which is needed to deal with unpredictable situations and to make decisions on the spot. And it takes manned aircraft to seek out unknown targets, to assess the damage achieved and to perform all other functions of reconnaissance. Without obtaining and exploiting all such information, strategic warfare becomes a costly, indecisive and hazardous guessing game.

Missiles are "one-shot" weapons, that is, they can be used only once, whether successful or not. In contrast, bombers can be recovered and "recycled," thus posing a continuing threat to the enemy.

Bombers are *proven* weapon systems, with a record of many millions of hours of operational employment in war and peace. SAC alone has flown its aircraft for some 20 million hours. Improvements and new equipment can be tested realistically and proved operationally in closely simulated combat missions. As a result, reliability figures are exceptionally high and, because of the innumerable data supporting them, can be used in war-planning without reservation.

Manned weapon systems are also more dependable than missiles, not only because of their greater reliability but also because air crews usually can deal with any malfunctions or emergencies that may occur in flight. And whereas some minor damage or failure may prevent a missile from reaching and hitting its target, World War II records show that crews of even badly crippled bombers managed to accomplish their mission. As one SAC planner put it, "There is no way to build guts into a computer!"

Manned weapon systems permit far more realistic training than missiles. Air crews actually fly the mission profiles they would have to follow in the event of war. Since SAC added the alternate tactic of low-level penetration, bomber crews have accumulated thousands of hours flying at the very low altitudes and over the type of terrain they would encounter on the way to their assigned targets. Bombing accuracy can be developed and tested with the aid of an ingenious system known as "Radar Bomb Scoring" (RBS). This system employs a radar signal that is triggered by the bombardier at the instant of "bomb release," and a ground receiving station which computes the accuracy of the "radar bomb." In contrast, only a small number of missiles can be launched for training purposes because of the very high cost involved. And no ICBM has ever been launched from an operational site.

SAC bomber crews include officers specially trained to operate complex "defense systems," a variety of countermeasures designed to "spoof" or negate an enemy's electronic bomber defenses. As it is not possible to predict exactly what defensive measures an enemy might use, at any particular time or location, the skill of an experienced defense systems operator is needed to employ any countermeasures best suited for prevailing conditions. But if the Soviets should develop effective anti-missile defenses, the countermeasures we could incorporate into our missiles would be limited to those designed for known defenses and known conditions.

If the Soviets should ever succeed in perfecting defenses against our missiles which we cannot overcome, any deterrent of ours that would be based primarily on missiles would no longer suffice to prevent aggression. We certainly must take this possibility into account since our survival demands that we prepare ourselves for any future contingency, regardless of how likely or unlikely it may appear at the moment. This means that we may have to fall back on our manned bombers which, at their altitude range, would not be vulnerable to antimissile defenses. For this reason alone it is mandatory that we not only maintain a modern bomber force but retain the capability to expand it again, at least until we would have found means to counter the Soviets' antimissile defenses. In fact, it is entirely conceivable that bombers someday may have to serve as penetration aids for our missiles by attacking an aggressor's missile defense system.

As long as there is a marked trend toward an all-missile deterrent in this country, the Soviets doubtless are encouraged to concentrate their efforts on antimissile defenses instead of spreading these efforts thin in trying to deal with the complex defense problems posed by our present mixed force. With such a concentrated effort, supported by their formidable scientific and industrial resources, the Soviets could well come up with some type of defense system which may greatly impair if not negate the effectiveness of our strategic missiles. No one can predict today whether such a system would employ antimissile missiles, exotic "beam" weapons such as an advanced form of "laser" beam, or perhaps a phenomenon as yet undiscovered. But it would be highly unrealistic and indeed irresponsible to claim that a reliable defense against missiles is "impossible" and that, for this reason, there will be no need for manned bombers in the future.

There is another important but seldom mentioned advantage of manned weapon systems. During periods of international crisis bombers on airborne alert or on special missions represent a clearly visible expression of national intent and demonstrate this country's determination and capability to protect its interests and those of its allies. Missiles in underground silos, within the confines of the United States, seem too remote and intangible to impress the average citizens of distant countries involved in local conflicts or crises. But the huge bombers patrolling the skies above or nearby can provide unmistakable warning to our foes and much needed encouragement to our friends.

For all these reasons I am convinced that the combination of manned and unmanned weapon systems, in a properly balanced and well coordinated mixed force, ensures a war-winning capability which neither can maintain by itself. The flexibility of this combination makes it possible to strike any number and types of targets, and to any extent necessary to destroy an aggressor's "capacity and will to wage war"; that is, to achieve a "military victory."

The Soviets do not have the capability to attain such a victory because of the unbalance of their forces and the system under which these forces operate. Nor will they ever have that capability as long as we endeavor to stay ahead of them and maintain our overwhelming superiority in strategic warfare. Therein lies our sole hope of deterring aggression indefinitely, and that is why we must always have a mixed force of strategic missiles and manned weapon systems—bombers and, eventually, manned spacecraft.

Many people who may agree "in principle" that there will be a continuing need for manned weapon systems express serious doubts that bombers can penetrate the sophisticated defenses of today, let alone those of tomorrow. These doubts, however, are normally not shared by men who have practical experience in bomber operations and are familiar with both the capabilities of our bombers and the nature of the Soviets' bomber defenses. While the Soviets have made great strides in their air defenses, SAC has made even greater strides in its penetration aids and tactics.

Ever since I began my flying career in 1928, I have heard people say that "soon" bombers would no longer be able to penetrate or would suffer such heavy losses as to make bomber attacks too costly. But to the best of my knowledge, no American bomber formation has ever been turned back or has been prevented from accomplishing its mission.

If someone had tried, in the early days of World War II, to predict the average attrition rate for tight formations of hundreds of bombers fighting their way through heavily concentrated flak and large numbers of fighters, he probably would have arrived at a very high estimate. Yet, out of a total of about 530,000 heavy bomber sorties flown during that war, only some 9500 aircraft were lost due to enemy action, for an average attrition rate of less than 1.8 percent.

I do not claim that bomber attrition rates in a nuclear war would be that low, but neither do I believe that they would be as high as is sometimes suggested. In trying to predict bomber attrition rates, one of the most important contributing factors is frequently overlooked, that is, the unpredictable factor of tactics. I maintain that the commander and his tactics, more than anything else, determine the losses in any offensive action. The flexibility in SAC's penetration tactics makes it possible to hold these losses to a minimum by affording a wide choice of strategies.

There are several other factors which should keep future attrition rates within acceptable limits despite continued improvements in the Soviets' aerial defenses. As these defenses become more sophisticated, they must rely to an increasing degree on electronic systems which, in turn, are more susceptible to electronic countermeasures and also more vulnerable. Moreover, attrition applies not only to the attacking forces but even more so to the defenses.

Throughout World War II, bombers generally disregarded the ground defenses because they were not considered worth attacking. However, if we should be forced into a nuclear war, the enemy's air defense system would become a priority target and would be attacked with the most effective penetration weapon devised by man—the hydrogen bomb. Each successfully dropped bomb would take out the defenses in a wide area and permit ever deeper penetration for successive bombers.

Penetration of enemy air defenses is further enhanced by the "Hound Dog" air-to-surface missile which, as explained earlier, can be used by the bomber to destroy the defenses many miles ahead in its path. Finally, ICBMs can be used effectively against certain types of defenses which would further assist in paving the way for the following bombers.

With such a variety of penetration aids and tactics, there can be little doubt that SAC's bombers would be able to accomplish their missions and do so at acceptable attrition rates. The numbers involved would be relatively small anyway because there will never again be a requirement for the huge bomber formations of World War II. The firepower concentrated in a single bomber today suffices to obliterate any target and, for that matter, several targets. Besides, missiles now can assume many missions formerly assigned to bombers.

But while we will need fewer bombers to maintain an effective mixed force, those bombers must be modern and advanced enough to meet the ever more stringent requirements of the future. In this respect the outlook is most discouraging although, up to my retirement, my civilian and military superiors generally supported the mixed-force concept. But many of them seemed to support it merely because they believed that this concept would have to be retained only until it could be supplanted by an all-missile deterrent force. This explains why, for the first time in the history of American strategic airpower, no follow-on bomber is under development.

The progressive deterioration of SAC's mixed force is reflected in the allocation of funds. In Fiscal Year 1962, SAC received about 13 percent of the defense budget. This figure had gone down to some eight per cent in Fiscal Year 1965 and may decline still further in subsequent budgets. Since a large percentage of military funds is spent to meet personnel expenses and support day-by-day operations, the drastic cut in SAC's share of the defense budget represents primarily the reduction in the procurement of new weapon systems. And, at present, the only weapon systems to be procured for SAC are those contracted for under long-established programs; that is, additional Minuteman missiles—no new bombers.

There has been and still is a great deal of talk and also much controversy about a new bomber for SAC. This problem has existed ever since the first B-52 became operational and the logical question of a follow-on for this bomber came up. I was still commander of the Air Research and Development Command, in the middle 1950s, when the contract for the development of the ill-fated B-70 was let. This aircraft was to fly at three times the speed of sound and incorporate some highly advanced bombing and navigation equipment. However, the B-70 program was plagued by so many technical problems and delays that it was "reoriented" several times. What had started out as a program for a new strategic bomber, became a "Reconnaissance-Strike" (RS-70) airplane and, finally, just a "test bed" for experimenting with the problems of flight at triple-sonic speeds.

What really "killed" this airplane, in my opinion, was the fact that it was designed for flight at very high altitudes which was very desirable at the time it was conceived. But this became a serious deficiency when the Soviets developed their present extensive system of high-altitude antiaircraft missiles. Therefore, current plans envisage a new bomber that would be capable of operating efficiently throughout a wide range of high *and* low altitudes.

Plans for such a bomber—designated "Advanced Manned Strategic Aircraft" (AMSA) at this writing—were still in the discussion and preliminary study stage when I retired and included features which I considered undesirable and a potential source of unnecessary problems and cost. But even if agreement had been reached on the desired characteristics and the decision were made today to award a contract for the development of this or any other new strategic bomber, it would take from eight to ten years until combat wings could be equipped with it. By that time, all B-47s would have long been retired; the remaining B-52s would be worn and obsolete, and the limited number of B-58s in SAC's inventory would be obsolescent at best. Thus, there would be a dangerous gap, and the gap keeps widening with every day a final decision for bomber replacements is postponed.

While still Commander in Chief of SAC, I submitted detailed recommendations for bridging this gap, without a crash program and excessive cost, in the hope that the supporters of the mixed-force concept will prevail in the end and efforts for maintaining a modern bomber force will be pursued with greater realism and vigor. My recommendations called for several types of manned weapon systems to serve different and overlapping time periods and thus avoid *any* gaps until a new strategic bomber would become available in operational quantities.

My first recommendation was to slow down the phase-out of SAC's B-47s. Even though the B-47 is an old airplane, it can help maintain SAC's combat readiness and prevent a serious decline in bomber capability until my second recommendation could be implemented.

This second recommendation was to procure additional wings of B-58 bombers. While SAC had some problems with its first B-58s—as is true for any new weapon system—subsequent modifications and improvements have made the B-58 a very fine and reliable aircraft which could fill SAC's medium-bomber needs for a number of years.

But since the B-58 became operational, the state of the art has progressed at a rapid pace, and it is doubtful that this airplane will be able to serve its purposes until the AMSA or a similar weapon system could be added to SAC's aging bomber inventory. I see one possible solution to this problem which may come as a surprise to many people, and that is to assign the new F-111 to the Strategic Air Command.

The F-111, which already has had its share of controversy as the "TFX," was designed as a fighter-bomber, as the letter "F" indicates. Actually, the F-111 possesses all the characteristics of an advanced medium strategic bomber; it will be able to do everything the B-58 can do, and will do it better. Production quantities of this aircraft are now on order and without added cost could serve to fill a most urgent strategic requirement, expeditiously and effectively. Moreover, the full strategic potential of this advanced weapon system can be exploited only by an organization which has an established capability in every phase of strategic air operations. SAC is the only organization in existence which has that capability.

In the interest of national security, the suggestion to assign the F-111 to SAC should be given the most serious and urgent consideration. Support for the Advanced Manned Strategic Aircraft is lukewarm, and the funds to be spent for the study phase are so small and uncertain that there is little likelihood of an early start of an actual development effort. In fact, there really is no assurance that this project will ever go beyond the study phase. This could mean that, by the mid-1970s, SAC may be virtually out of the bomber business and this nation will no longer have a mixed strategic force to ensure superior strike capability.

If this should come to pass, I am convinced that, eventually, the need for new bombers will become so apparent and pressing that a crash program would have to be initiated in order to rebuild the bomber force as well as the organization required to operate it. But in view of the fact that it took so many years and such extraordinary efforts to develop the SAC organization to its present peak of efficiency, it would seem almost hopeless to try to rebuild it fast enough once it has been disbanded. The addition of the F-111 to SAC's bomber inventory would, at the very least, serve to keep this organization intact and help maintain a bomber capability which it will always be easier to expand than to rebuild from scratch.

I had another recommendation which I would like to mention because it combined many of the advantages of both the manned and unmanned weapon systems. Briefly, I suggested a long-endurance aircraft that could remain on airborne alert for extended periods of time and would be large enough to carry a sizable number of missiles, either ballistic missiles similar to the

Minuteman or air-breathing guided missiles similar to the Hound Dog or both. Patrolling outside the range of enemy radars and countermeasures, such an airborne missile-launching platform would be even safer from attack than the Polaris submarine and far less expensive. Putting it differently, just as the Polaris submarine uses the oceans of water to protect its survivability, the airborne-alert missile platform would use the still more abundant oceans of air.

The development of such an airplane would not require time-consuming and expensive advances in the present state of the art and could, therefore, be accomplished quite rapidly and cheaply. Limited quantities of this aircraft would greatly contribute to the credibility of our deterrent and further enhance the flexibility of the mixed force. With a choice of missile types on each aircraft, the airborne ballistic missiles could be employed against normal strategic targets while the air-breathing missiles, which can either fly high or hug the ground, could be used against future bomber or missile defenses. No action has been taken on this recommendation.

In weighing the merits of these and any other recommendations for strengthening and ensuring SAC's strike potential, it must always be remembered that the primary purpose of all our deterrent tools is to make the need for using them in anger as unlikely as possible. Therefore, decisions should not be made on the basis of what *we* want and what we should buy so as to keep everybody happy. We must be guided solely by a realistic assessment of what will keep the Soviets and any other aggressor nations convinced, five and ten years from now, that we would defeat them decisively in any war they may force upon us.

In my considered opinion, the recommendations which I have discussed above offer the greatest promise in this respect. I can only hope that a sufficient number of our citizens will agree with these recommendations and see to it that they will be incorporated in the nation's design for survival before it is too late.

When we speak of "deterrence" in the context of national survival, we normally think of deterrence of nuclear war. And when we speak of the "tools of deterrence," we usually refer to the nuclear strategic forces which, through the threat of retaliation, constitute the keystone of the nation's deterrent posture.

Therefore, in discussing our tools of deterrence, I have limited myself so far to the capabilities, operations and problems of the Strategic Air Command which, initially, was the only military organization equipped with nuclear weapons and devoted entirely to the conduct of strategic air warfare. While the latter still holds true, SAC is no longer the only "nuclear-capable" strike force in this country although it still represents some 90 percent of the Free World's nuclear firepower.

Continued advances in nuclear technology have permitted the production of nuclear weapons in greater quantities and smaller dimensions, thus making them available for use on medium-sized aircraft and missiles. As a result, the nuclear strike capability of SAC now is being shared, to an increasing degree, by that of fighter-bombers, carrier-based aircraft and submarines. All these weapon systems are under the operational control of the commanders of the U. S. forces in various geographic areas throughout the world and, with the exception of the Polaris submarines, serve primarily the overall geographic mission of these commanders. The Navy's Polaris submarine now is the only nuclear weapon system outside of SAC which is designed specifically for strategic operations and, therefore, is a "tool of deterrence" in the sense of deterring general nuclear war.

For a limited time, there were two other weapon systems which fell into this category, namely, the Thor and the Army-developed Jupiter Intermediate-Range Ballistic Missiles (IRBM). Designed for shorter ranges and, hence, considerably smaller than the ICBMs, Thor and Jupiter missiles were deployed in England, Italy and Turkey, with the United States maintaining control of the nuclear warheads and SAC providing support and training.

This program was phased out by 1963 for a number of reasons, but primarily because of the increasing vulnerability of the Thor and Jupiter as purely retaliatory weapons. They were standing unprotected above ground and, as the Soviets acquired a considerable inventory of IRBMs of their own, could be easily destroyed in a surprise attack. Moreover, their reaction capability was slow, by today's standards, because of the time necessary for fueling and installation of the warhead prior to launch.

In contrast, the Polaris program has been extremely successful and grown into an important contributor to the nation's military deterrent. The name "Polaris" actually refers only to the solid-fueled missile employed in what is officially designated as the "Fleet Ballistic Missile Weapon System." Besides the missile itself, this system consists of a nuclear-powered submarine, which in effect is a mobile launching site, and all necessary support facilities at sea and on shore.

Nuclear submarines can travel vast distances without surfacing, as was demonstrated spectacularly by the USS *Triton* in 1960 when it cruised around the world submerged in 84 days, covering over 40,000 miles. When "on station," the nuclear submarine remains on its far-ranging underwater patrol for long periods of time and can launch its missiles while submerged.

The first Polaris submarine—to use the popular term—was deployed operationally in November 1960. Only four years later the number of deployed FBM submarines had increased to 21 and was growing rapidly, with a presently programmed total of 41 to be operational by 1967 at the latest. There are two complete crews of about 130 officers and men for every submarine so that a large percentage of the ships can be on station at all times. The cost of the nuclear-powered submarine is over $100 million which does not include the cost of the missiles, tenders and other support facilities.

Each FBM submarine carries 16 Polaris missiles of which there are three generations: the A-1 with a range of 1,200 nautical miles, the A-2 which has a range of 1,500 nautical miles, and the A-3 which covers 2,500 nautical miles. The first five Polaris submarines were equipped with the A-1 missile but will be converted to the more advanced A-3 which will also be carried on the last 23 ships in the program. All missiles have small but powerful nuclear warheads.

The Polaris system has proved very reliable in extensive tests, has rapid reaction capability and, above all, is practically invulnerable because, roaming the expansive depths of the oceans, it can readily escape detection and enemy action. All these qualities make the Polaris an excellent strategic weapon system which already plays a vital role in the nation's nuclear deterrent force. Target selection and assignments are made under the "Single Integrated Operational Plan" which will be explained in the next chapter.

By the time all 41 projected Polaris submarines have become operational, with an average of 34 deployable at all times, there will be over 500 missiles in that fleet alone which could be launched against an aggressor on short notice. Some proponents of the Finite Deterrence concept have suggested that this would suffice to maintain a credible deterrent, obviating the need for bombers and land-based ICBMs in the future. Such a suggestion is highly unrealistic because it disregards some crucial factors.

In the first place, we can no longer afford to "put all our eggs in one basket," whether these eggs be bombers, ICBMs or Polaris submarines. If we were to do so, we would permit the Soviets to devote their entire defense effort to combatting a single type of weapon system which would greatly simplify their task and enhance their prospect of success. And if they should succeed in devising effective measures against such a single type of weapon system in our inventory, we would no longer have any deterrent at all.

While the Polaris weapon system has excellent survivability at present, we must not rule out the possibility of future advances in the Soviets' anti-submarine warfare which would make our submarines vulnerable to yet unforeseeable methods of detection and attack. In this connection, it must be realized that the Soviets can test any new detection methods, even in peacetime, against the Polaris submarines themselves and can thereby ascertain beyond any doubt whether these methods are effective or not.

Another potential impairment of the Polaris system's future effectiveness lies in the possibility that the Soviets may eventually perfect antimissile defenses which could prevent the Polaris missiles from reaching their targets. While these possibilities may seem remote at this time, they must be taken into account in our planning for the future, regardless of the kind of deterrent strategy we may choose to pursue.

The advantages of a mixed force of bombers and ICBMs are enhanced by the addition of the Polaris submarines. The integrated combination of these three entirely different types of strategic weapon systems gives us very high assurance that our deterrent cannot be wiped out, from one day to the other, by some dramatic technological breakthrough on the part of the Soviets. Moreover, this combination lends strength and credibility to a deterrent that must have unmatched flexibility, superior striking power and war-winning capability in order to be and remain effective.

These, then, are our principal tools of deterrence today. They ensure a safe "deterrent margin" for the present and the immediate future. I have little doubt that they can do so indefinitely, provided we make certain that we always have the quality, quantity and variety of tools we need to meet future threats, and especially any potential threat from space.

But as is true for any other tools, the sophisticated and powerful tools of deterrence must be wielded by craftsmen if they are to produce what they were designed to produce—lasting peace in a free world. We can achieve this objective as long as our tools of deterrence are adequate and are used by our statesmen and elected leaders with skill, wisdom and firmness.

9. The Deterrent System

IN military terminology a "weapon system" is defined as a major weapon, such as a bomber or missile, *plus* all the specialized support facilities, equipment and devices required to operate and maintain that weapon. In the broader sense, a complete weapon system also includes all necessary personnel as well as the facilities to support and train them. The difference between these two terms lies in the fact that a weapon by itself has no military value; only the complete "weapon system" is capable of accomplishing the mission for which the weapon is intended.

By the same token, the tools of deterrence cannot deter by themselves, no matter how sophisticated and self-sufficient they may be. They must be part of what I call a "Deterrent System" in which each component, in cooperation with all others, contributes to an overall objective. This objective is not merely deterrence of nuclear war, although this is the most urgent mission, but deterrence of any kind of aggression, whether military or non-military. And just as deterrence of military aggression requires a credible war-winning capability, we can meet any other types of aggression only through a similarly convincing capability of the Deterrent System to win any phase of the cold war.

For deterrence is not a goal in itself; it can contain Communist aggression but it cannot defeat the Communist ideology which must be our ultimate goal if we are to survive as a sovereign nation. To achieve this goal requires offensive action— and I do not mean military action—while deterrence is essentially defensive. However, deterrence if successful will keep the playing field open so that men of good will everywhere have the time and freedom of action to work for what the late President Kennedy envisioned as "a peaceful world community of free and independent nations—free to choose their own future and their own system, so long as it does not threaten the freedom of others."

It is evident, therefore, that the Deterrent System goes far beyond the preservation of the "deterrent margin" which is merely a measure of *military* superiority. The Deterrent System encompasses many other factors, both tangible and intangible, which either support the military component of overall deterrence or serve the exigencies of the cold war. Nor is the Deterrent System limited to national aspects. In a world divided into two camps, with many nations straddling the fence, the contributions of our allies represent an important factor in our common struggle against Communist aggression and expansionism.

I have the impression that the interrelationship and interdependence of all these factors are not always well understood by our citizens and have not been given sufficient attention in our design for survival. For this reason, I want to discuss some of the principal aspects of our Deterrent System, pointing out the strengths which I feel we should preserve as well as the weaknesses which should be corrected.

Turning first to the military aspects of the Deterrent System and, specifically, the deterrence of general nuclear war, a major problem, which was created by our expanding nuclear capability, is the relationship of the diverse "nuclear-capable" strike forces which came into being as a result of the production of nuclear weapons in larger quantities and smaller sizes. However desirable the growth and diversification of our nuclear capability were, they did not proportionally increase the nation's overall nuclear strike potential because they led to some unavoidable duplication of functions and conflicts regarding areas of responsibility.

The ensuing problems were so far-reaching from the standpoint of national security and their solution so significant that I considered it important to bring this matter to the public's attention and, therefore, discussed it extensively in both official and informal talks. Nevertheless, I feel that the complex problems involved in nuclear teamwork still are not sufficiently understood.

To begin with, the overlapping military capabilities brought about by advancing technology are not, of necessity, undesirable. They are certainly preferable to gaps, especially where such overlaps add to our total fighting strength. On the other hand, overlapping functions can prove wasteful and indeed harmful unless strict control can be exercised in the assignment of distinct areas of responsibility. This applies, in particular, to the increased nuclear capabilities throughout our military establishment.

As long as this entire capability was within one command, namely SAC, coordination of all planning and operations pertaining to the employment of nuclear weapons presented no problems whatever. SAC Headquarters had the sole responsibility for every phase of targeting and mission assignment which not only assured optimum utilization of our then relatively limited nuclear resources but also precluded any duplication and conflicts in strategic air operations.

This was no longer possible when military units outside of the Strategic Air Command attained nuclear strike capability. These units are assigned to the various "unified commands" which are charged with combat operations in a specific geographic area, such as the Atlantic, Pacific and Europe. The unified commands are composed of elements from all services, as required for operations in their particular area. In contrast, the Strategic Air Command is global in nature and composed of Air Force personnel only. SAC, which is called a "specified command," and the unified commands are under the operational control of the Secretary of Defense through the Joint Chiefs of Staff.

It is important to understand these lines of authority because the commanders in chief of the unified commands prepare individual war plans for their organizations, in accordance with overall policy provided by the Secretary of Defense and the guidance of the Joint Chiefs of Staff. As the war plan of each unified command is concerned strictly with operations in its assigned geographical area, there is little likelihood of conflicts with the operations of other unified commands. However, since SAC's operations are global, conflicts did arise with SAC's war plan once the various geographic commands achieved a measure of strategic nuclear capability.

These conflicts were not merely a matter of overlapping missions. As the unified commands engage in a variety of land, sea and air operations in their specific areas, their newly acquired strategic task became only one of many and, therefore, served primarily in support of the geographic mission rather than the nation's overall strategic mission. As a consequence, the strategic operations provided for in the war plans of the unified commands not only entailed frequent duplication and even triplication of SAC operations but actually tended to impair the accomplishment of SAC's mission.

The routing and timing of SAC's bomber sorties are so intricate and complex that electronic computers must be employed to calculate such factors as precise time over target and proper spacing between bombers to insure maximum mutual support with minimum interference. As increasing numbers of missiles were added to SAC's operational inventory and were assigned targets in SAC's war plan, their timing had to be carefully scheduled also. No such detailed schedules were possible for the new strategic support operations of the unified commands in the various geographic areas. The ensuing problem facing SAC was similar to that of a railroad which runs carefully scheduled trains over its lines and, all at once, finds other trains using its trackage without any schedule.

Apart from the wastefulness of unnecessary mission duplication, there was now the danger that one American airplane or missile might blow another out of the sky over enemy territory. Once these problems were recognized, steps were taken to alleviate them. A system was established by which the commands concerned would hold so-called "world-wide coordinating conferences," designed to coordinate their war plans so as to eliminate duplication and interference in strategic air operations. However, these conferences failed to achieve their purpose, primarily because it proved difficult if not impossible to resolve, through committee action, the many basic differences that developed. Still more difficult to cope with was the factor of time.

Preparation of a detailed war plan is a long and involved task that takes many months to accomplish. Once that plan has been completed, it must be submitted to and approved by the Joint Chiefs of Staff, which takes additional time. Thus, by the time the approved war plans of the individual commands could be submitted to the coordinating conferences and attempts had been made to resolve existing differences, as had to be done in the past, these plans were no longer current. War plans require regular updating because of revised requirements, changes in matériel or deployment, new intelligence and related factors.

Several approaches were suggested to improve on the inadequate system of worldwide coordinating conferences. Suggestions ranged from proposals for revising existing coordinating procedures to establishment of a "United States Strategic Command." This Command was to incorporate all forces possessing a nuclear strategic capability, including SAC, and was expected to provide, on an all-inclusive scale, the same centralized control of nuclear planning and operations as was exercised by SAC when it was the only nuclear force.

The then Secretary of Defense Thomas S. Gates realized that the mounting coordinating problem called for bold and urgent action, and he therefore decided to effect a compromise between the widely differing solutions advocated by the three military services. This compromise entailed the organization of a "Joint Strategic Target Planning Staff" under the Joint Chiefs of Staff, which Mr. Gates called "the most important decision I have participated in since I have been in the Pentagon." The new agency was formally established in August 1960 and was given a twofold task, namely, the preparation of both a "National Strategic Target List" and a "Single Integrated Operational Plan" for all our strategic strike forces.

The Secretary of Defense further directed that the Joint Strategic Target Planning Staff, which came to be known by its initials "JSTPS," be located at the headquarters of the Strategic Air Command, at Offutt Air Force Base, and he appointed me, in my capacity as the head of SAC at that time, as its director. The reasons for this action are obvious. SAC was, as it still is today, by far the largest nuclear force in the Free World and, moreover, maintained at its headquarters the most extensive targeting and intelligence facilities for strategic operations in existence.

Because of the unified nature of this nuclear team, the Secretary of Defense provided that the deputy director of the JSTPS be a general or flag officer from another service. Up to my retirement, three Navy vice-admirals served successively in this position. The working staff is composed of a relatively small number of carefully selected officers from the Army, Navy, Marine Corps and Air Force who are experts in the various weapon systems and operations covered by the JSTPS. They develop the nuclear operational plan in conjunction with representatives of all participating unified commands and are supported by SAC's own Intelligence and Operations personnel.

One innovation of the greatest significance to the Deterrent System of the Free World was the addition, in 1964, of NATO officers from West Germany, Italy, the United Kingdom and France as representatives of the Supreme Allied Commander in Europe. While the JSTPS is concerned directly only with the general war plans of the United States nuclear strike forces, the NATO representatives are kept current of our planning as it affects their own operations and thus can assist, on a day to day basis, in coordinating NATO's war plans with ours.

The working staff of the JSTPS is divided into two groups.

The first group is charged with the preparation of the National Strategic Target List which, in essence, defines the job to be done. This task involves the development of target systems for any number of contingencies and for any combination of potential aggressors within the entire Communist bloc. Thereby, it provides the basis for the work of the second JSTPS group.

That group has the task to work out the Single Integrated Operational Plan for the effective employment of all available strategic forces against the various target systems and under a variety of conditions. This is accomplished in accordance with the "National Strategic Targeting and Attack Policy" which is established by the highest authorities in Washington and spells out our national military objectives in general war. (It is noteworthy that, at the time of my retirement, this Policy still entailed the preservation of strategic superiority and war-winning capability although not enough was being done to ensure the achievement of the Policy's objectives in the future.)

The effective and timely accomplishment of the two JSTPS tasks required one more provision—the director was given the authority to resolve any disagreements that might arise within the staff. Therein lies the fundamental difference between this organization and the worldwide coordinating conferences, for the work of the JSTPS staff is never hampered or delayed by unresolved disagreements. But the authority which the director was given is not absolute because he must bring any major areas of disagreement to the attention of the Joint Chiefs of Staff who have the right to overrule him. From my own experience as director I can state that this provision acts as quite a "restraint" as proven by the fact that, during my entire tenure, there was not a single case in which the Joint Chiefs of Staff had to overrule my decision.

It is natural that disagreements should arise because each branch of the service, each arm and each major command have their own requirements and have evolved their own modes of operation to meet these requirements. To integrate their plans and operations into one common mission frequently meant concessions on their part which seemingly were disadvantageous to their own missions. I am happy to say that, in my over four years as director, the members of the JSTPS staff have always subordinated service loyalties and personal preferences to the demands of the national nuclear team. Their extraordinary efforts represent real unification in action.

The importance of these efforts can best be gauged by a brief summary of what has been accomplished. The first National Strategic Target List and Single Integrated Operational Plan were completed and approved by the Secretary of Defense in December 1960—less than four months after JSTPS was established. They were implemented in the spring of 1961 and now are being revised on a regular basis so as to keep our strategic strike forces provided with up-to-date operational plans which reflect the latest targeting information and force structures.

It is difficult to convey a picture of the complexity and scope of these plans whose paperwork alone weighs some nine tons. They not only involve innumerable details, but all these details must be fitted together with painstaking accuracy, tying the operations of thousands of globally deployed elements into one vast integrated and mutually supporting team action. All this complexity, however, is in one place only, namely, within the JSTPS at SAC Headquarters. There is little complexity about the end products that are forwarded to the Joint Chiefs of Staff and Secretary of Defense, and to the forces in the field.

The JSTPS provides, in effect, "packaged plans" which give the President of the United States a wide choice of options to meet any contingency and affords him complete flexibility regarding any action he may decide to take for the employment of the nation's nuclear strike forces in response to aggression. Once he has made his decision, he merely transmits the appropriate code to the field, and the particular war plan he has chosen will be put into effect immediately. Not a minute will be lost in getting off that vital first counterstrike, to whatever extent and in whatever area or areas the President has selected, because all these contingencies have been taken into account in the various options at his disposal.

Nor does the JSTPS entail any complexity for the forces in

the field. It furnishes detailed mission instructions to all operating elements included in the common plan—the Polaris submarines on station, the SAC bombers and missiles on alert, the fighter-bombers overseas, the carriers at sea. Once the President has given the order and designated the option he has selected, all combat crews will know exactly when and where to go and what to do.

It should be emphasized that all this applies only to the initial counterstrike in a general nuclear war because no one can predict the situation after the initial exchange accurately enough to permit the preparation of one common overall war plan for subsequent operations. Moreover, as a planning staff, the JSTPS has no operational control over the forces represented in it, and its Single Integrated Operational Plan in no way affects the other operations of the unified commands. Therefore, they are in the position to pursue freely their assigned geographic missions both during and after a nuclear exchange as well as in any local crises and conflicts in their respective areas.

The only weapon systems under the operational control of unified commands which have strictly a nuclear strategic mission are the Polaris submarines. For this reason, the Single Integrated Operational Plan is written primarily around SAC and Polaris, with all other nuclear-capable strike forces under the unified commands assigned supporting strategic missions contingent on their availability for such missions.

There can be no doubt that the very existence of an integrated nuclear team has lent added weight and credibility to our strategic deterrent. It is particularly gratifying that the invaluable benefits derived from the JSTPS in that respect entailed no added cost to the taxpayers and that, virtually with the stroke of a pen, the nation's nuclear striking power has been strengthened immeasurably. For the first time, this country has a common plan for general war, with a common strategy and common timing, and a well-functioning machinery is now in existence to keep this plan absolutely current at all times.

I have dwelled on the Joint Strategic Target Planning Staff

at some length because it is a striking example of how our Deterrent System can be enhanced merely through improvements in the management and relationship of its components. Conversely, the Deterrent System can be weakened greatly if unwarranted organizational changes should impair the future utility of the JSTPS. This explanation of its operations and mission applied at the time these lines were written. There is no assurance, however, that this will continue to apply if current trends toward a purely defensive nuclear deterrent should bring about major changes in military force structure.

But even if we should retain our present concept of deterrence through superior and war-winning strategic power, there will be continued need for modifications and improvements in the implementation of this concept which may also affect the JSTPS. While its creation represented a tremendous step forward at the time, only future developments can show whether it went far enough and whether still greater centralization in the management of our strategic forces will become necessary in the years ahead.

As military technology advances at an ever increasing pace, new weapons and methods of warfare may be developed that may revolutionize military strategy and tactics to an even greater degree than resulted from nuclear weapons and missiles. Current concepts of land, sea and air warfare may well become obsolete, profoundly affecting the traditional missions and roles of the military services. No one can predict what dramatic changes in military organization this will entail, but regardless of service tradition and sentiments we must always be ready and willing to make whatever changes may be required to improve the effectiveness of the Deterrent System.

The question has been raised whether the nuclear component of our Deterrent System, that is, the strike forces represented on the Joint Strategic Target Planning Staff, does not afford far more nuclear firepower than we will ever need. The Strategic Air Command in particular has been accused of planning to "overkill" its targets, allegedly to justify its requests for more bombers and missiles. It may be appropriate at this point to try to put the myth of the overkill to rest, once and for all.

The overkill argument has its roots in statements in the literature and press by various "experts" to the effect that our strategic strike forces, of which SAC is the major component and "culprit," program more weapons against their assigned targets than are needed to destroy them. The point is made that one single nuclear bomb or missile warhead suffices to obliterate any target and that sending more than one nuclear weapon against a target constitutes wasteful "overkill," that is, planning destruction where there is nothing left to destroy.

Using the same logic, one might say that it is wasteful to put more than one pellet in a shotgun shell because, after all, one pellet in the heart of a duck or pheasant is enough to kill it and there is no sense in trying to kill it more than once. Of course, the sole reason why there are several dozen pellets in a shell is to increase the probability that at least one of them will find its mark. If the hunter could predict with absolute assurance which of the many pellets would be the fatal one, he could leave all the others out of the shell and save himself some money. But he does not know; all he knows is that the multitude of pellets in his shell improves his chances of success. While it is still possible that none of those pellets will hit his prey, it is normally more likely that more than one will hit it.

This is essentially the principle that governs the targeting of our nuclear weapons, although the numbers involved are far smaller. In trying to determine the type and number of weapons to be programmed against any particular target system, the JSTPS planners cannot be guided by hopes and assumptions; they must make as certain as possible that these weapons will destroy "the aggressor's capacity and will to wage war" and convince him that this is precisely what would happen should he force war upon us.

This means that the officers who prepare the Single Integrated Operational Plan of the JSTPS must always ask themselves two questions: What probability of destruction is required for any particular target, and how can this probability be achieved? Without going into details, it should be explained that the various targets that would have to be attacked under specific conditions are arranged in order of priority, with the highest priorities assigned to those targets which pose the greatest threat to American lives and property, and to our allies. It stands to reason that, the higher the priority of a target, the greater must be our confidence that we can destroy it if we must. In other words, the desired "kill probability" for any target is established on the basis of its priority rating.

Once the planners have ascertained what degree of assurance is required for the destruction of a target, they must determine the type and number of weapons to be programmed against it. Toward this end they "war-game" each weapon system that is being considered for this mission, all the way from pre-launch to detonation of the warhead. They take into account the possibility that this weapon system may be destroyed before it can be launched, its chances of abort, unfavorable weather conditions, enemy action, duds, misses, and any other factors that may cause the mission to fail. In this manner, the planners arrive at the probability, expressed in terms of a percentage, for a particular weapon system to destroy a particular target to the degree desired.

Let us assume that, in a specific case, the kill probability of a missile has been calculated to be 50 percent, which means that chances for success and failure are exactly even. If the target does not warrant a higher kill probability, only that one missile will be programmed against it. But if the target demands a higher kill probability, at least one more weapon must be programmed. Assuming again—strictly for the sake of simplicity— that each of the two weapons has a kill probability of 50 percent, mathematics show that their combined kill probability is not 100 percent but 75 percent. If a still higher assurance of success is required, it is necessary to program additional weapons. (I should mention that this entails the use of different weapon systems and tactics which have different kill probabilities. Because of their variety, they seriously compound an enemy's defense problem in addition to improving overall chances of mission success.)

It is true that, if it takes several weapons to achieve a kill probability of, say, 90 percent, it is conceivable—although highly improbable—that all would hit the target and "overkill" it. But there also remains a ten percent probability that none of them will hit, leaving a potentially very dangerous target intact. Hence the expressed concern about "overkilling" and "needless waste" is utterly unfounded and based on a lack of understanding of the vital difference between a *programmed* weapon and a *delivered* weapon.

It is this difference which explains why any realistic war plan requires more weapons than would be needed if there were assurance that each and every one would destroy its assigned target. This is not a matter of waste and "overkill" but of giving substance to our deterrent and, if deterrence should fail, of minimizing our losses and the danger of defeat.

We are playing for the highest stakes there are, the survival of our nation, and we cannot afford to leave the success of the most important military factor in our Deterrent System to chance and wishful thinking.

In addition to the nuclear strategic forces, the military component of the Deterrent System comprises all of the other forces in the Army, Navy, Marine Corps and Air Force. This includes also the trained men in the reserves and National Guard. The Deterrent System, as previously defined, goes beyond the deterrence of general nuclear war, which is primarily the task of the nuclear strategic forces, and hence demands superior military strength in every aspect of modern warfare.

This is the more important as we are in a retaliatory role which means that the initiative lies with the Communists and that they are normally the ones who choose the locale and timing as well as the type and scope of military action in which we may have to engage. As a result we never know when, where and how they may plan to strike, and we can hope to deter them from doing so only as long as we manage to convince them that we are prepared *and* determined to meet and defeat them anywhere and anytime, and in any kind of conflict. That is the reason why we need credible superiority across the *entire* spectrum of warfare on land, at sea and in the air.

Of equal importance to our Deterrent System is superiority in defense, especially defense against a missile attack. As I pointed out earlier, the Soviets are not likely to risk a deliberate missile attack against this country unless two conditions are met: one, they must be convinced that they can keep the damage to be expected from our retaliatory attack within acceptable limits and, two, they must be confident that their attack will achieve the desired result, that is, inflict such decisive losses on us as to force our surrender.

To meet the first condition, the Soviets must either neutralize most or all our retaliatory forces, which is virtually impossible with our present mixed force, or perfect reliable defenses against our strategic bombers, ICBMs and Polaris submarines. And to be confident that they can meet the second condition, the Soviets must be certain that *we* have no effective defenses against their land-based and submarine-launched missiles.

I have little doubt that the Soviets are making an all-out effort to develop the best possible missile defenses while our effort in that area has left much to be desired. Consequently, we have no defense whatever against missiles today and the status of our work with antimissile missiles makes it unlikely that we will have an effective missile defense system in the near future. Similarly, I do not think that we are spending enough effort toward major advances in antisubmarine warfare while it appears reasonable to assume that the Soviets are trying their best to cope with our Polaris submarines.

I believe that the development of adequate defenses against missiles and missile-firing submarines should be given high priority, not only because of their deterrent role but, even more so, because of the lives they would save if deterrence should fail. I am confident that we have the brains as well as the facilities in this country to solve the crucial defense problem, provided it is given the attention and funds it deserves.

With regard to our offensive capability other than strategic, I fully concur with those who call for strong conventional forces to deal with local crises and conflicts because, after all, one cannot liberate anyone with a hydrogen bomb. But I do not agree with the often heard claim that our conventional forces have been neglected because "most of the defense moneys went to SAC and the other nuclear forces." SAC's share in the defense budget, which was 13 percent in Fiscal Year 1962, continues to decline. The figures for the nation's entire strategic nuclear deterrent went from about 18 percent of the defense budget in 1962 down to some ten percent in Fiscal Year 1965 and are likely to decrease considerably more in future budgets. Hence, over 80 cents out of every defense dollar have been available for purposes other than strategic nuclear strike capability, and that figure has been and still is going up steadily.

It is, of course, true that not all of this 80-plus percent can be spent for limited-war capability. A large share must go to support activities, personnel services, air defense, research and development, administration, training, and the innumerable other phases essential to the management and operation of a large military establishment. But the point is that any alleged problems with our limited-war forces certainly cannot be attributed to lack of funds caused by "excessive" cost of the general-war deterrent.

I have the impression that there is some fuzzy thinking regarding the extent of conventional capability that is really required. The question should not be: how big a conventional force do we need to fight limited war, but how big a limited war do we intend to fight with a conventional force? In other words, there is little sense in arguing about requirements for conventional forces and weapons until we have decided on the maximum scope and type of armed conflict we desire or can afford to fight with them.

Would we fight another world war with the weapons of

World War II and rather be defeated by superior enemy forces than make discriminating use of the best weapons we have? Would we consider another Korea, which cost us over 150,000 casualties in some three years of indecisive fighting, a mere local conflict that should again be left to the limited-war forces to settle?

Obviously, we will have to make up our minds as to what we consider a "limited war" to be fought with limited-war forces and from what point our national interests demand the use of our strategic strike forces as well as the use of some nuclear munitions. Once we have agreed on what that point should be, we must let all potential aggressors know, including the Red Chinese and their little friends. There can be no more effective deterrent against deliberate expansion of local wars than the certain knowledge on the part of our enemies that this would force us to go beyond the use of conventional weapons.

I fully recognize the problems involved in such a policy and will discuss them in some detail in the following chapter. But as far as our Deterrent System is concerned, it is my considered opinion that the conventional forces we now have in being are adequate for any size and type of limited war which can and should be fought with such forces. Therefore, I see no present need to expand them, especially if this is done at the expense of our capability for general nuclear war as current trends indicate.

Moreover, considerable amounts of money have been and are being spent for the development and procurement of modern equipment for the limited-war forces. This is a wise and necessary investment, and I hope that this modernization process will be continued.

In particular, I would like to see the addition of one or more nuclear-powered aircraft carriers which I am convinced would immensely strengthen our limited-war capability as well as our overall Deterrent System. While the primary role of carriers is their leading part in local crises and conventional conflicts, they also have an important capability for nuclear war which is utilized effectively in the Single Integrated Operational Plan of the

JSTPS. (The opposite is true for SAC whose primary mission is deterrence of nuclear war but which also has a secondary or supporting capability for conventional and limited war.) A nuclear-powered carrier, which in an emergency can stay at sea for very extended periods of time and has many other operating advantages, would be especially well suited for this dual role and, therefore, greatly enhance the striking power and versatility of our carrier fleet.

I also feel that the moneys expended for providing the Army with modern tactical aircraft are well spent as long as this does not lead to unnecessary and harmful duplication of the tactical air missions of the Air Force and Navy. The Army requires certain aerial functions over which it should have direct control as they are essentially extensions of operations on the ground. On the other hand, aerial support of ground troops—strafing of enemy concentrations, bombing of fortifications, interdiction of supplies going to the front, and maintenance of air superiority —is and should remain the role of the Tactical Air Command of the Air Force and, where in range, of the Navy's carrier-borne aircraft.

The semantics involved in trying to resolve the conflicts between the expanding tactical role of Army aviation and that of the Air Force and Navy fighter-bombers must be rather confusing to the public. This confusion is compounded if, in addition, it is attempted to define the difference between *tactical* and *strategic* air missions, and I think that it was a serious mistake to ever establish this distinction. When fighter-bombers attack strategic targets—military installations, marshalling yards, supply depots, industrial complexes—hundreds of miles deep in enemy territory, they are no longer carrying out their primary mission of close-in ground support but are conducting strategic missions. I maintain that such missions can be accomplished better, more economically, more effectively and safer by long-range strategic aircraft operating from bases far beyond the reach of the enemy.

But all these problems really are not as serious as they may seem to the people directly involved. They stem from the fact that, as military technology advances, capabilities of the various branches of the armed forces expand commensurately which is bound to create some areas of overlapping functions. Therefore, it becomes necessary from time to time to redefine the roles and missions of the military services and their major components so as to keep step with changing conditions.

I feel that slow but definite progress is being made in that respect, despite the frequent criticism that there is too much "unnecessary duplication of effort" and "wasteful competition" within the armed forces. Although some of this criticism may be justified, it is not always understood that, in an establishment as vast and complex as the military, a certain amount of duplication is unavoidable, if not actually desirable. Nor is it appreciated that there are many areas in which the individual services cooperate to the fullest degree and are engaged in joint or unified efforts. The most important examples are the unified commands, which are responsible for all combat operations in specified geographical areas, and of course the JSTPS.

It has been my experience that, as a rule, the military services have managed to work out any conflicts between them because their responsible officers realize that they all have a common objective and can best achieve this objective if they work together as a team. For this reason I do not agree with those people outside the military who insist that there is need for more, or perhaps complete, unification of the armed forces.

I feel very strongly that the identity of the individual services should be retained because there is already too much overall centralization within our military establishment. Basic roles and missions are accomplished most effectively and economically if they are assigned to a military service which, by tradition and character, is best qualified to perform such roles and missions. Also, a reasonable degree of competition between the services is healthy because it engenders greater efficiency, progress and esprit de corps. Therefore, unification should be limited to joint efforts in those areas where centralized control and management are conducive to the overall military objective.

There are all too many people who immediately want to change an organization the moment problems arise, instead of making certain first that, whatever deficiencies they may see, are the fault of the organization rather than of persons in responsible positions within that organization or of the manner in which it is being used. Thus, there are persistent voices who call for radical changes in the organization of our military establishment just because they disapprove of certain policies or features which have little bearing on the effectiveness of the organization itself.

I have had ample opportunity to observe and experience directly both the strengths and weaknesses of the various concepts of military organization that prevailed throughout my military career. It is my conviction that the present organization of our military establishment is entirely adequate, at least under the conditions which exist today.

The authoritative position of the Secretary of Defense, who manages the military establishment in behalf of the Commander in Chief—the President of the United States—assures strict civilian control which I consider mandatory for any military forces, and especially in a democracy. The Secretary exercises direct operational control over the unified and specified commands—the major combat elements—through the Joint Chiefs of Staff, which is composed of the military service chiefs and a military chairman. In this manner, the Secretary can count on competent professional advice and assistance in the implementation of his policies and directives. In turn, the civilian chiefs of the services—the Secretaries of the Army, Navy and Air Force—are responsible to the Secretary of Defense for the management and administration of the services under their direction and thus provide the necessary support for the combat functions.

All of this is very well thought out and, in my opinion, has proved itself. It makes the President the Commander in Chief of the armed forces not only in name but in fact, as it should be. His powers in that capacity are clearly defined by the Constitution and properly balanced by those of the Congress which thus can make certain that the President's decisions and actions are in accord with the will of the majority of the people.

I see no way of improving on these principles of command and control even though individual citizens or groups of citizens may quarrel with some of the policies and actions of the prevailing civilian management because of political considerations, personal convictions or a host of other reasons. That is desirable also since it leads to open discussion of all vital issues in which the people should take an active interest. If they do not approve of the manner in which their will is being carried out, it is certainly within their power to change it.

But while the basic principles of our present military organization and chain of command appear very sound, I have found that there is room for improvement in some of the methods of operation. In particular, I have noted a marked tendency toward increasing centralization of operational functions and details within various Defense Department staff offices which were established originally to deal solely with the formulation and implementation of policy, as directed by the Secretary of Defense. This assumption of operational functions has lessened the authority of the commanders in the field without lessening their responsibilities and has adversely affected both their effectiveness and prestige.

I realize that the tremendous power and implications of nuclear weapons require tight and central control over all military elements charged with the custody and potential employment of these weapons, and that this control must be exercised by the appropriate civilian authorities. On the other hand, these authorities must have enough confidence in the professional competence of military commanders to merely tell them *what* to do and not tell them *how* to do it. If the problem is one of lack of confidence, the field commander concerned should be replaced with someone who merits sufficient confidence in his professional qualifications and judgment to leave the execution of policy directives and operational orders to him.

But, again, these and related problems are of a relatively minor nature and can be easily corrected once there is mutual agreement on the desirability or need of doing something about them. What really counts is the fact that our present military establishment, on the whole, is meeting the demands of the Deterrent System and can be counted upon to accomplish its diverse missions successfully—today. We are fortunate indeed that we have the means and talent to make certain that this will be equally true in the future.

The Department of Defense has the responsibility for another important phase of the Deterrent System which, although designed primarily for the civilian population, is closely related to military preparedness—civil defense.

Unfortunately, the civil defense program has not been given the wide public support and cooperation it deserves, which may be due to a number of reasons. Some of our citizens seem to feel that in the event of nuclear aggression, destruction would be so widespread and thorough that it would be futile to try to save anything. Others consider the possibility of nuclear war too remote to justify the expenditure of large sums of money for shelters and other civil defense measures. Others again simply do not care or object in principle to anything that has any connection with war. In fact, there has been considerable opposition to any civil defense effort on the part of people who believe that it would be "provocative" and might be construed by our enemies as preparation for a pre-emptive war.

To correct such misconceptions and complacency the public must be made to understand that civil defense has two vital functions. First, it impresses on potential aggressors that our deterrent is not a hollow threat and that we are both prepared and determined to fight back if we are attacked. Thus, instead of being "provocative," civil defense actually adds to the credibility of our deterrent.

Second, there is always the possibility that, despite the most effective Deterrent System, we may get involved in a nuclear war. This could occur, for instance, as a result of inept diplomacy or a miscalculation which may cause the inadvertent escalation of some local incident. Also, we may fail to maintain an adequate "deterrent margin" and thus encourage rather than deter Communist aggression.

Therefore, we cannot rule out the possibility that we may be forced into a nuclear war, and as long as that possibility exists, no matter how remote, we cannot afford to disregard it in our design for survival. If this threat should ever materialize, a timely and well-planned civil defense program would accomplish two objectives—it may save tens of millions of lives, and it would expedite our recovery, thereby ensuring the preservation of our national integrity.

Because of lack of interest and understanding, the civil defense program got off to a slow start and underwent several reorganizations which did not suffice to coordinate and properly support the many scattered civil defense efforts and activities throughout the country. Finally, in August 1961, a Presidential Executive Order placed civil defense under the Department of Defense which, subsequently, designated the Army as the principal agent for providing support.

I considered this action a major step forward. In fact, I had long advocated that the Army be charged with the responsibility for civil defense because of the conviction that a nation-wide effort of this nature should be under military direction. The Army in particular has the necessary command structure, organization and facilities to support an effective civil defense system and, in the event of an actual attack, assume emergency control.

The civil defense program could be further enhanced, without added cost, by making more extensive use of the experience and skills represented in our reserve forces. While some provisions have been made toward that end, I believe that it would be most beneficial to assign larger numbers of reservists from all services to civil defense duties in their hometowns, both for operational functions and training. This would not only permit them to meet their active-duty commitments in a more gainful manner than is often the case now but would also help foster wider understanding and support of civil defense on the local level.

Although it is not within the purview of this book to go into the details of the civil defense effort, such as the shelter program and related projects, the quality and scope of this effort have a direct bearing on several aspects of our deterrent strategy which should be pointed out. I mentioned earlier the role of civil defense in strengthening the *credibility* of our deterrent. Another aspect is the potential effect of a comprehensive civil recovery plan in preventing the Soviets from reaching the decision that a surprise attack on this country will achieve the desired results. If we can convince the Soviets that such an attack would not render us helpless and that we could recover from its effects faster and better than they could recover from *our* retaliatory strike, they would be further discouraged from risking costly aggression.

For this reason, representatives of business and industry, public utilities, labor unions and similar organizations must continue to work closely with the Office of Civil Defense and the appropriate state and local authorities in implementing our comprehensive national plan for emergency operation, mutual assistance and joint programs for expeditious recovery. Again, such a coordinated plan has not only deterrent value but is also of immeasurable benefit in a real emergency.

The industrial recovery potential especially represents an important factor in our overall deterrent. Beyond this, industry as well as science contributes a major share to the continuous improvement of this deterrent. As I stated before, the tremendous striking power of the Strategic Air Command is in the hands of a relatively small number of people—the 19,000 men in the aircraft and missile combat crews. What gives them this power is not merely the organization and the 250,000-odd other personnel supporting them, but the modern weapons which science and industry have provided—the nuclear weapons, the aircraft, the missiles. If these 19,000 men were armed with bows and arrows, their striking power would be negligible, regardless of their skill and courage and the organization behind them.

This is equally true for all other combat elements, the personnel who man the modern guns and tanks, the aircraft carriers and submarines, the interceptors and fighter-bombers.

In this technological age we could never stay ahead in the race for military superiority unless we have technological superiority, and that is where our science and industry have done a superb job. As the head of the Air Research and Development Command and, later, of SAC, I got to know many of the nation's leading scientists, engineers and manufacturers. I was always greatly impressed with their competence, helpfulness and, above all, keen awareness of their demanding responsibilities in helping to maintain and strengthen the country's deterrent power. And I always found them receptive to my suggestions and occasional criticisms some of which I want to mention because of their broad significance.

One of my most frequently voiced demands was for ever greater reliability of our weapon systems. In my dual capacity as a war planner and the head of SAC, I stressed reliability more than any other quality because it is a critical factor in providing the necessary degree of assurance that priority targets will be destroyed. If reliability is poor or uncertain, more weapons must be programmed against a target system, which is wasteful and reduces target coverage.

I realize that, in a complex new weapon system composed of thousands upon thousands of components, it is extremely difficult to obtain the reliabilities which can be expected and demanded of proven weapon systems, such as bombers, which have been brought to virtual perfection through years of operational use. But it has been my experience that our scientists and engineers are capable of increasing overall systems reliability dramatically if project managers give quality control priority over minor improvements and any other considerations. We need continued improvements also, but reliability must come first if the weapon systems in our current operational inventories are to serve their day-to-day deterrent mission.

Related to this problem is the tendency toward unnecessary complexity in both weapon systems and support equipment.

Such complexity not only reduces reliability but also increases cost and the lead times for development and testing. It is true that modern technology permits the accomplishment of functions which human minds and hands could never perform or not perform as well. But there are other functions which men carry out as well or perhaps even better and more dependably than automatic devices, and there may be some functions which are not at all necessary for the achievement of a particular mission or objective.

It is natural for scientists and engineers to strive for ever greater sophistication and automation in the equipment they design or contract for. But I think it may be well to exercise more discrimination in weighing the resulting advantages against the disadvantages of increased complexity. This should be borne in mind when the military establish requirements which may cause more complexity than is desirable or even necessary for the desired purpose.

On the other hand, I see an urgent need not only for quantum advances which lead to steady and major improvements in performance but also for technological breakthroughs that may have a profound effect on the very character and techniques of future warfare. Because of the ever accelerating pace of technological advance, the next ten years conceivably may bring even more rapid and dramatic progress in weaponry than we have witnessed during the past decades. Indeed, there may be weapons or perhaps techniques of waging war, from the depths of the oceans to the far reaches of space, which are as much beyond anyone's imagination today as were the hydrogen bomb and supersonic airplanes when I flew my first bombers.

The demanding task ahead of our science and industry is to make certain that we, not our enemies, will always be the first ones to reach any new plateaus of technological advancement. I am confident that they can achieve this objective as long as they do not concentrate their efforts on the exploitation of known principles and concepts to the exclusion of dynamic programs for the exploitation of radically new approaches and fields. Such programs will yield double benefits, because the discoveries which are bound to be made will not only help us maintain military superiority but, in the long run, will also benefit our civilian economy and standard of living.

A prosperous industry and sound economy as well as scientific competence in all disciplines contribute far more to our overall Deterrent System than the means and tools to maintain our military deterrent at an adequate level, without impairing our way of life. They are also indispensable weapons in fighting the cold-war phases of Communist aggression by giving the nation the strength and stability to maintain its leadership in any field of endeavor and thereby help stem the tide of Communist expansion, through peaceful means.

No one can predict for how long we will have to keep up this all-inclusive deterrent posture. To ensure the preservation of that deterrent for as long as we may need it—perhaps indefinitely—we must have the best possible schools, colleges and universities, and there have been too many words and too few actions in this respect. The Soviets have shown far greater appreciation for the importance of a superior educational system to the achievement of their objectives. While we need not emulate their autocratic methods, we certainly have the means and talent to surpass the Soviets and anyone else in the quality and scope of their educational programs. We must never forget that our institutions of learning help shape the most vital asset for our future—the young men and women who someday will have to carry on our efforts of protecting the nation's welfare and survival.

There are, of course, many other factors and aspects which contribute, directly or indirectly, to our capability to deter aggression and to counter any attempts, from without or within, to impair or destroy that capability. But there is one more factor that plays a rather unique and not always recognized role in our Deterrent System, and that is the nation's public media.

The public media perform three tasks which I consider of the greatest importance to the continuing success of our deterrent. Their first task is to keep the public informed of the nature and scope of the threat we face and of the steps that are taken or should be taken to meet that threat. Serving as the primary means of communication between the government and the people, the public media promote public understanding and, thereby, public support for the needs of defense.

The second task is to help convince our enemies that we have both the capability and determination to destroy them, if they should attack us, and to protect our national interests and those of our allies, if they should try to impair them. The public media reflect the sentiments of the American people, and any potential aggressor who analyzes these expressions will find that the great majority of our citizens will brook no infringement on the nation's interests. Nor should there be any doubt that we have the means to protect these interests. Therefore, I do not share the concern of some people that our public media disclose too much military information, although I agree fully that such information must never compromise classified data and subjects. We cannot expect to deter anyone by hiding our strengths. If we want to impress our enemies—and encourage our friends—we must let people throughout the world know of our strengths, and the public media are the most effective means for doing so.

The third task of the public media is to provide a nationwide forum for the frank and open discussion of all controversial issues relating to the principles, strategies and means of preserving peace. It is essential that our citizens not only learn what these vital issues are but also be informed of all conflicting views so that they can make an intelligent choice. I have enough confidence in the American people to be certain that, as they ponder their choice in such issues, sound logic will stand up.

In my opinion, the nation's public media are performing all three of the above tasks in an outstanding manner, despite some often-heard criticism that they tend to be inaccurate, too sensational or speculative, and occasionally too prejudiced in their accounts of defense policies and military matters in general. But when published information is incorrect or wrongly interpreted, the fault sometimes lies with the source.

I have met a great many representatives of the "fourth estate" and have found almost all of them responsible and competent persons who were anxious to give their readers or listeners an accurate and thorough report on the status and demands of national defense. But I was restricted in the amount and type of information I could provide, primarily for reasons of essential military security. Similar restrictions apply, of course, to all interviews with military personnel.

Beyond this, however, there may be political or international considerations which can have considerable bearing on the type and extent of military information released by the civilian authorities at any particular time. It is, therefore, not surprising that reporters and commentators are tempted to fill in any gaps by drawing their own conclusions and to make assumptions which may not be accurate or are influenced by their personal convictions.

Freedom of the press is one of the most important prerequisites in a democracy. But freedom in this context refers not only to the right of expression; it must also include the right of information, to the full extent permitted by the demands of national security.

The Deterrent System, which has been discussed in this chapter, is directed against all forms of Communist aggression and, therefore, must serve not only this country but all free nations threatened by the Communists and, especially, our allies with whom we have mutual assistance pacts. Conversely, our allies make certain contributions to the Free World's Deterrent System, and it may be well to examine to what extent these contributions aid our common objectives.

As the acknowledged leader of the Free World, the United States has helped create an interlocking network of international alliances and collective security pacts which encompass nations in every part of the world. The deterrent value of this globe-circling network stems primarily from the fact that a Communist attack on one member of an alliance would be considered an attack on all other members and, conceivably, on the entire network of alliances. Although few if any of these alliances could cope with Communist aggression successfully without the assistance of the United States, the very fact that this country participates in or supports an alliance helps to deter aggression against any of its members.

The most extensive and far-reaching alliance within the Deterrent System of the Free World is the North Atlantic Treaty Organization (NATO) which was formed in 1949 for the common defense of Western Europe and now comprises 15 nations, including the United States and Canada. The strength of NATO lies in its well organized and closely integrated military organization which is composed of land, sea and air forces placed under its control by the member nations. The joint military effort has brought about closer relationship and cooperation in other areas which, in turn, has greatly strengthened the political significance of the NATO alliance. Thus, stretching from the United States and Canada in the West to Turkey in the East, NATO represents an imposing bulwark against Communist aggression and expansionism.

As the largest and most powerful member, the United States is called upon to make the greatest overall contribution to the NATO alliance. This is recognized by the fact that the Supreme Allied Commander, with headquarters in Paris, always has been an American, although important command positions within the sprawling organization have been fairly divided among the participating countries. The United States carries the major share of NATO's financial burden—over 70 percent —and provides most of its nuclear capability.

But in my opinion, our most important contribution to NATO is the retaliatory power of our own nuclear strike forces which serves to deter aggression not only against the United States but also against any of our allies. The Single Integrated Operational Plan of the Joint Strategic Target Planning Staff is coordinated with NATO's war plans so as to ensure the most effective utilization of all our nuclear resources. It has been questioned, however, whether the NATO-controlled share of these resources has added sufficiently to the overall nuclear deterrent to make it worthwhile.

There has been and there still is much controversy on both sides of the Atlantic regarding the value of NATO's nuclear strike capability and the desirability of expanding it further, for instance, through the establishment of a "multilateral nuclear force" as proposed by our government. The point has been made that the U. S. nuclear strike forces—principally SAC and the Polaris fleet—already possess enough weapon systems and nuclear weapons to cover all essential targets in the entire Sino-Soviet bloc, even under the most unfavorable conditions. It has also been argued that the Soviets doubtless have sufficient numbers of Intermediate-Range Ballistic Missiles to attack all military targets in the European NATO countries and that, with tactical warning reduced to a very few minutes at best, NATO's strike forces would have little chance of surviving a surprise attack.

All these points may be well taken, but I believe that the whole question of NATO's nuclear capability is too complex to permit an unequivocal answer. It is true that, in the event of nuclear aggression, this capability may have relatively little military significance and poor survivability. On the other hand, NATO's nuclear strike forces do pose a substantial threat to an aggressor and, therefore, would have to be attacked, thereby increasing and compounding the Soviets' strategic problems. Hence, the very existence of these forces adds more to the overall deterrent than their potential operational value may indicate.

Nor do I agree with those people who object to the expansion of nuclear capability within NATO on the grounds that the "proliferation" of such capability is undesirable and endangers the peace. In my opinion, this argument is rather unrealistic because it fails to take into account that there will be proliferation, and increasingly so, whether we like it or not. Communist China has already exploded a nuclear device, and several smaller countries reportedly are making progress along that line, with others sure to follow. Only the United States and Soviet Russia had the immense resources required to develop nuclear technology, but this technology now is firmly enough established and its principles are well enough known to permit countries with lesser resources to develop and produce nuclear weapon systems. Considering the tremendous military and political advantages of such weapons, there can be no doubt that nations bent on, or threatened by, aggression will make every effort to obtain them, one way or another.

As long as we must anticipate that, eventually, a growing number of nations will have some measure of nuclear capability, we certainly should permit and even help our allies to be among those nations. After all, we want our friends to be strong and at least match the strength of comparable nations in the enemy camp. That is why I considered it beneficial to our cause when President de Gaulle undertook to create a French nuclear strike force, despite the concern and criticism voiced by his own allies. There is no telling what will happen when other Communist nations in addition to Soviet Russia and Red China come into the possession of nuclear weapons, and there will be problems when more and more of our friends achieve nuclear capabilities of their own. But the problems with our friends can be easily resolved to mutual satisfaction—as long as they are and remain our friends.

This brings me to another issue which deserves some thought, and that is the stability of the NATO alliance and, for that matter, of any of our present alliances. There has been much talk about the decay of the "monolithic" structure of global Communism because of its split into the Moscow-led faction and the faction led by the Red Chinese. But little has been said about the problems besetting the monolithic structure of the Free World. The Soviets and Red Chinese still agree on their ultimate objective—to "bury" the democracies, and especially the United States. They differ only in the methods they propose to employ. In contrast, the countries of the Free World often fail to agree even on their objectives because, in many of these countries, national objectives may vary drastically and suddenly in accordance with internal conditions and politics.

This has caused some inevitable problems and changes in our alliances, with more in the offing. In NATO, France under President de Gaulle has been more difficult to deal with than under his predecessors and shown increasing inclination to go its own way. Greece and Turkey, two of NATO's most valued nations, almost got into a war over the Cyprus issue—ironically both being armed predominantly with American weapons—which might have forced them to withdraw their forces from NATO. Italy, another important NATO nation, has the largest European Communist Party outside the Bloc and would undoubtedly leave NATO if, at any time in the future, the Communists should gain control of the government.

The Baghdad Pact of 1955 became the Central Treaty Organization (CENTO) when Iraq, after the overthrow of its West-oriented government, abandoned the alliance with Iran, Pakistan, Turkey and the United Kingdom. (The United States is not a member of CENTO but supports it actively.) And Pakistan, which is also a member of the Southeast Asia Treaty Organization as is the United States, has shown bitter resentment over U. S. aid to its enemey India and may, eventually, be pressured into leaving both alliances.

The Organization of American States (OAS) has been troubled with the Communist activities of Cuba which owed its very independence to us, yet turned into a bitter enemy and caused the scuttling of our Monroe Doctrine. Some other members of the OAS, subjected to Cuba-directed subversion and revolutionary activities, may change their unstable governments and join the Communist camp.

Thus the character and composition of alliances keep changing constantly, as friends become enemies and enemies turn into friends. This is by no means a new phenomenon. Take, for instance, our allies and enemies in World Wars I and II. In World War I, Italy and Japan were on our side, Turkey fought with the enemy; these roles were reversed in World War II. Germany was our enemy in both wars; now West Germany, the greater part of the old Germany, is one of our staunchest allies. Russia was our ally in both wars, but if there should be another world war, it would undoubtedly be our principal enemy and supported by a number of nations who used to be our allies in World War II, while Italy and Japan would probably be on our side.

The lesson to be drawn from all this is that we must never permit our design for survival to become so dependent on any alliance that, if it should fail us, we would fail also. This does not mean that alliances are worthless simply because they may not last indefinitely. We must make every effort to establish and maintain as many alliances as we can, regardless of the material contribution such alliances can make to the Free World's Deterrent System. For every nation in our camp is one less nation in the Communist camp, and the more uncommitted nations we can induce to join us, the better will be our prospect of containing the Communist scourge.

But as has been true throughout the past decades, it will be up to us to carry the main load in the continuing struggle for peace in a free world. Even if the day should come, sometime in the future, when Communism will no longer be a threat and, like so many other aggressive ideologies, will have spent its force, we still will not be able to relax our deterrent posture.

The military threat of Communism, for which our present deterrent is designed, actually is relatively recent because it did not pose a danger to our survival until several years after World War II. It was no issue at all in that war because we had to fight an entirely different threat, the threat posed by the aggressiveness of the Nazis, the Fascists and the Japanese war lords. And a different threat again had forced us into World War I when we fought the imperialism of the Central Powers and resolved to "make the world safe for democracy."

The point is that if and when Communist aggression should no longer be a threat, there will be other threats and other ideologies and other nations or alliances bent on aggression. It may be a China with its own brand of Sino-Communism, engulfing the entire Far East and threatening the life lines of the

Western nations, perhaps including European Russia. Or, some generations hence, it may be an African Hitler, pitting the potential power of that continent against Europe, or a South American would-be Napoleon casting greedy eyes on North America.

We are blessed with more riches and enjoy a more abundant life than any other nation in the world, and that is why we will always be the prime target for the aggressive designs of any future dictator or ill-conceived ideology. We must anticipate this in creating a Deterrent System that can be adapted to any future conditions and threats. Most of all, this deterrent must always be based on our own resources and our own capabilities and our own control, regardless of any prevailing alliances.

The Deterrent System we have in being today essentially meets these conditions. It has many strengths but also many weaknesses. Whether the strengths will prevail over the weaknesses depends on the one factor that ties all the diverse components together—man. But this is another story, and another chapter.

10. Some Issues of Limited War

SINCE the end of World War II, this country has been involved in a number of widely scattered local crises and armed conflicts which constituted serious enough threats to our national interests to warrant our intervention. As a result, there has been widespread public concern for the implications of limited war which, because of its various controversial aspects, has engendered much academic discussion and many popular misconceptions.

"Limited war," in its generally accepted sense, is merely one phase of the total conflict between the free and Communist worlds. The spectrum of this conflict may range from seemingly minor crises all the way to general nuclear war, and the term "limited war" is applied rather loosely to any type of military involvement on our part which lies somewhere between the minimum and maximum intensities of possible actions. The point is that all these actions, while varying in intensity and scope, are part of the overall Communist offensive against the Free World and, therefore, should not be treated as separate issues requiring different policies of approach.

I have the impression that this premise is not too well understood because many people, who seem to take it for granted that the problem of general nuclear war now is fairly well under control, insist that we should turn to a different policy and

217

a different set of strategies in coping with the problem of limited wars. In my opinion, this proposition fails to take into account the nature and objectives of limited war as a Communist tool.

We used to define "limited war"—often called "local war" or "brushfire war"—as any localized military conflict in which the United States and the Soviet Union support, directly or indirectly, opposing sides without being officially at war with each other. The Korean war is the prime example of such a conflict. But this simple definition is no longer valid since the Red Chinese have started to support local actions on their own without relying, as previously, on the back-up or at least the tacit approval of their erstwhile Soviet comrades-in-arms. In fact, the Chinese-supported rebel activities in South Vietnam and Laos did not suit the Soviets at all, and when the Chinese invaded Indian territory the Soviets even continued to provide some military equipment to India.

It would, therefore, seem that the original definition of limited war should be extended to any localized armed conflict in which the United States supports one side while the Soviet Union or Red China or both support the other side. But the whole problem of limited war has become far too complex to make even this broader definition inclusive enough. For instance, it would not cover the curious fact that, in the Indian-Chinese border conflict, unusual circumstances found the United States and the Soviet Union supporting the same side.

It must be realized that the Soviets normally foment and support local conflicts for somewhat different reasons than apply to the actions taken by the Red Chinese. The Soviets do not necessarily instigate local conflicts but, wherever conflicts arise for one reason or another, they shrewdly choose the side most suitable for their purposes and support it with diplomatic actions and military equipment, goading us into supporting the other side. Their purpose in fomenting crises and armed conflicts in every part of the world is to keep us off balance and sap our strength, thus enhancing the achievement of their ultimate goal—global Communist domination under their leadership. Using the expedient of limited wars, in addition to their cold-war tactics, they endeavor to achieve this goal without confronting us directly and without the heavy cost of general nuclear war.

The Red Chinese, in contrast, do not direct their limited-war ventures specifically against the United States although they consider us their principal enemy. Their primary objective is to bring all of Southeast Asia under their direct control. It is in the pursuit of this objective that they either undertake aggression themselves or foment and support local wars, guerrilla warfare and rebel activities. As these actions are directed against nations with which we have collective security pacts or whose independence is of vital importance to our national interests, we are becoming involved in such conflicts, and increasingly so as the military capability and audacity of the Red Chinese keep mounting.

In addition to the various *types* of limited war there is also the matter of *scope* and *intensity*. Limited war is not a clear-cut matter such as general nuclear war in which all the military resources of the West would be pitted against all the military resources of the Communists. Our involvement in a local conflict may be limited to financial aid and the supply of military equipment. Or we may go further and provide "military advisers" who may take an active part in hostilities, as became necessary in South Vietnam. This may lead to direct action by elements of our armed forces against the enemy of the side which we are supporting, as was the case in August 1964 when North Vietnamese torpedo boats repeated their unprovoked attack on the U. S. destroyer *Maddox* in the Gulf of Tonkin. Finally, we may find ourselves in a full-fledged war, involving considerable numbers of U. S. forces and large amounts of matériel, as happened in Korea. (The fact that we acted in behalf of the United Nations in this case had more political than military significance.)

In trying to establish our military requirements for dealing with all these varieties of armed conflict, we must also take into account our needs for handling crises that are likely to develop into limited war. Such crises entail a host of diplomatic actions and declarations of intention which may have to be supported by the actual deployment of forces. We may have to do so in the defense of a friendly nation, as we did in the Lebanon and Quemoy crises, or for our own protection, as was necessary when the Soviets placed nuclear missiles on Cuba.

It is, therefore, evident that the term "limited war" encompasses too large a variety of special situations and armed conflicts to permit a precise and all-inclusive definition. Moreover, any attempted definition would apply only to this country because any action that may seem localized or limited to us may well be total war to the nation or nations directly concerned—and vice versa. For that matter, an all-out war involving only the United States and the Soviet Union (sometimes referred to as "central war") or Red China or both could be construed as "limited" by all other nations, regardless of whether such a war would be fought with conventional or nuclear weapons.

For all these reasons it is rather misleading to speak of "limited-war forces" as opposed to "general-war forces" because such differentiation would imply that there are two distinctly different kinds of conflicts and that, in each case, one type of force must be used to the exclusion of the other. It is equally misleading to differentiate between forces for "conventional war" and those for nuclear war because the so-called conventional forces may have to use nuclear munitions while the forces usually considered as "nuclear"—such as the Strategic Air Command—may employ conventional, that is, non-nuclear weapons.

With all this complexity and confusion, it is extremely difficult to determine the type and quantity of forces we need to adequately cover the entire spectrum of conflict in which we may have to engage, from local crises to general nuclear war. As I have emphasized repeatedly, this determination must be made on the basis of two factors, namely, the assessment of the overall threat and the strategy or strategies necessary to meet that threat. But as these factors are subject to individual interpretation, especially with respect to limited war, there is wide disagreement in the conclusions, and I consider this one of the most critical controversies in our entire design for survival.

I am particularly concerned about the growing conviction that the Soviets can be deterred from nuclear aggression by a limited number of missiles and that they will, instead, resort increasingly to "wars by proxy," that is, brushfire wars which they instigate or foment and support but not directly engage in. It is this reasoning which has led to the widely accepted conclusion that we must place ever greater emphasis on the forces required to fight such wars.

And this is exactly what the Soviets want us to do! The more we weaken our nuclear deterrent, the greater would be the intensity and scope of limited war the Soviets could allow and help to develop without risking escalation into nuclear war. And the more effort we expend in trying to deal with every possible type of crisis and conflict, the more we will scatter our strengths and drain our military and economic resources. In other words, we would play the game entirely by the rules the Soviets try to establish. Certain basic principles must be understood by the American people if we want to avoid being tricked into a game of Russian roulette.

First and foremost is the principle that we cannot afford to become involved in any kind of crisis or limited war except behind the shield of an overwhelming nuclear deterrent based on a credible war-winning capability. Without that shield, we cannot risk participation in any conflict that may lead to direct confrontation with Soviet or Chinese forces because we could no longer deter escalation into general war and, therefore, would not have the freedom of action necessary to resolve crises and limited wars in our favor. This means that our primary emphasis must remain on our nuclear deterrent. I am sure that this can be accomplished without impairing our limited-war capability.

Second, before getting involved in a crisis or armed conflict, we must make up our minds regarding the essential objective we want to achieve. Once we have decided on that objective, we must make every effort to attain it and be willing to employ all the military strength and weapons that may be needed toward that end.

Third, once we are involved in an armed conflict that continues to drag out and expand, we must establish the maximum scope and intensity beyond which we can no longer afford to limit ourselves to conventional methods and weapons.

Fourth, it is the avowed policy of this country to deter any kind of war, and there is no reason why we should not use the same basic principle for deterring limited wars that we have used for the deterrence of general war. That principle is to keep any potential aggressor convinced that the price of aggression would be far higher than he might be willing and able to pay.

Fifth, the strategy employed in deterring or conducting limited wars must be based on a realistic assessment of the threat in each particular case. But, as is true in the deterrence of general war, such assessment becomes a matter of conjecture unless there is sufficient "hard" intelligence, an area in which we have been dangerously deficient.

Some of the reasoning behind the above principles is self-evident or has been discussed previously. But there are a few more points which should be considered in trying to establish the parameters of an adequate capability for dealing with limited wars.

Despite their close political relationship, general nuclear war and limited war differ in some important respects. We cannot fight a general nuclear war on our own terms unless we initiate it which, of course, is highly unlikely. On the other hand, we have more latitude in a limited war because we can normally decide when and where to join it and to what degree to participate in it. Also, to meet the threat of nuclear aggression, we must be prepared to react with little or no prior warning while we may have days or even weeks to prepare for limited-war action.

Furthermore, the only issue at stake in general nuclear war is our survival and our only objective, therefore, must be total military victory. In contrast, limited war permits limited objectives and even compromises if it is mutually desired and advantageous to terminate it. Finally, we can make up for mistakes or a miscalculation in a limited war of limited objectives, but we cannot afford to make any mistakes in general nuclear war because we would have neither the time nor opportunity to make up for them.

All this permits the conclusion that it is neither necessary nor feasible to create a limited-war capability which would match Communist strength in men and matériel all around the globe or which would allow massive deployment of land, sea and air forces to any number of trouble spots at the same time. What we really need, in my opinion, is a reasonable number of well-balanced and diversified tactical forces, equipped with superior weapons and matériel and highly trained for the various specialized tasks which we are liable to encounter in limited conflicts.

I maintain that we have the diversity and numbers of forces needed to deal with any type of limited conflict, now and in the foreseeable future, and that we have the means to dispatch such forces expeditiously by air or sea wherever they may be required. Since we can control the time and scope of our involvement in limited war, we can deploy any additional forces at the speed permitted by our air and sealift capacity. And if more forces should be considered necessary than are readily available, they can be drawn from the reserves and National Guard both of which are trained essentially for conventional war and, time and again, have proved tremendous assets in national emergencies.

However, I can see no reason for permitting any limited conflict to expand into a vast military operation and drag out indecisively for months or even years, as happened in Korea. Falling into the Communists' trap, we have let ourselves be tricked into protracted wars of attrition which modern weapons have made militarily unnecessary. Protracted limited wars, such as the conflict in South Vietnam, have become prohibitively expensive, drain military strength and, because of our lack of success, make our deterrent for both nuclear and limited war less credible.

I believe that, beyond a certain point in an indecisive limited conflict, we should either pull out under the best possible conditions or should utilize the conventional capability of our strategic strike forces to "persuade" the aggressor to abandon his aggressive actions and objectives lest he pay an increasingly higher price for them.

It appears to me that we can use the principle of "persuasive deterrence" in bringing limited wars and local aggression to a swift and satisfactory conclusion, with minimum expenditure in lives, matériel and cost, and without excessive drain on our military resources. Let me explain the application of this principle by using as an example the situation in South Vietnam as it existed at the time these lines were written.

Trying to assist an unstable government and strifetorn nation against Communist aggression, masterminded by Red China, we found ourselves in another protracted conflict that was costly in men and matériel, with little promise of an early and acceptable solution. The military problem as I saw it, stemmed from the fact that we attempted—and unsuccessfully so—to help counter the widespread guerrilla activities of the Communist rebels instead of stopping these activities by cutting off all the support the rebels were receiving at its source— North Vietnam or Red China or both. This could have been accomplished by various methods, and I shall describe a hypothetical operation to explain one of these methods.

Let us assume that, in the fall of 1964, we would have warned the Communists that unless they ceased supporting the guerrillas in South Vietnam, we would destroy a major military supply depot in North Vietnam. Through radio and leaflets, we would have advised the civilian population living near the depot of our ultimatum and of the exact time of our attack so that civilians could be evacuated. If the Communists had failed to heed our warning and continued to support the rebels, we would have gone through with the threatened attack and destroyed the depot. And if this act of "persuasive deterrence" had not sufficed, we would have threatened the destruction of another critical target and, if necessary, would have destroyed it also. We would have continued this strategy until the Communists had found their support of the rebels in South Vietnam too expensive and agreed to stop it. Thus, within a few days and with minimum force, the conflict in South Vietnam would have been ended in our favor. Beyond this, we would have gained immeasurably in prestige and in the credibility of our determination to prevent further Communist aggression against our allies.

All this would have been achieved without a major offensive against North Vietnam and the sizable forces required for such an operation. The aerial attacks would have been undertaken by a few bombers of the Strategic Air Command, operating from their regular bases. Attacking at night and guided by radar, the SAC bombers would have been virtually invulnerable to any countermeasures available to the North Vietnamese. And carrying large payloads of conventional bombs, they would have destroyed their assigned targets with the utmost accuracy and discrimination.

This operation would have been carried out without the assistance and deployment of any other forces on the ground or in the air, and would have been accomplished within less than a day after SAC had received the order. Moreover, SAC would have undertaken these missions without any augmentation of its resources and would have done so without the slightest effect on its alert posture for the deterrence of general nuclear war.

I realize that many people in this country would have objected to such an operation even though it would have prevented further sacrifices in American lives—not to mention matériel and cost. Their main argument would have been that such a strategy of "persuasive deterrence" might have led to the direct participation of Red China and, conceivably, to an inadvertent escalation of the South Vietnamese conflict. But Red China, in 1964, was in no position to risk direct confrontation with the United States. Nor could there be any doubt that the Soviet Union would have limited its assistance to propaganda and halfhearted diplomatic support. In fact, the Soviets would probably have welcomed a setback in the uninhibited and reckless ventures of the Red Chinese comrades.

I have used the example of this hypothetical case not only to explain a possible solution to drawn-out, costly and indecisive limited wars, but also to point up the potential value of strategic airpower both in helping to win local conflicts and in reducing the need for large-scale tactical operations. This does not mean that strategic airpower is a substitute for tactical operations in limited war. There will always be a requirement for specialized forces to deal with specific problems—counterinsurgency forces to combat guerrillas; Navy and Air Force fighters and fighter bombers for maintaining air superiority and providing close-in ground support; Marines to conduct amphibious operations; and many others.

But strategic airpower can and should be used more extensively to complement all these forces and thus help keep their numbers to a reasonable level. For instance, SAC bombers should be employed for destroying major fixed targets. This would not only assist ground operations but, where such targets might otherwise have to be assigned to less suitable tactical aircraft, would free these aircraft for tactical missions.

Again, I may be accused of being partial to the Strategic Air Command because of my long association with it. But, in my opinion, strategic air operations have become so firmly associated with general nuclear war and "massive retaliation" that their usefulness in helping to deter and win limited wars tends to be overlooked. An objective analysis will show that long-range airpower has a number of features that make it uniquely useful in limited conflicts.

Long-range strategic airpower can be applied against any target on earth within a few hours and on short notice, as was demonstrated in the previously mentioned Operation Order Blank in which eight SAC bombers from different bases were dispatched against targets in widely separated parts of the world and carried out simulated bombing attacks on these targets within a few minutes of each other. There is no requirement for logistics other than routine aerial refueling, nor for lines of supply, augmentation of forces, building of forward airstrips, or any other costly and time-consuming preparations. All of this makes the use of strategic airpower extremely economical and simple. Also, it can be withdrawn and re-applied as often as necessary or desired which is not feasible with large tactical forces because, once withdrawn from an area of limited conflict, they cannot be redeployed to that same area without major difficulties.

Finally, the use of strategic airpower in limited war has a most significant political advantage. It can be applied without stationing a single American military man in the country which we are supporting or near the country we are fighting. In contrast, the employment of ground forces and short-range aircraft requires large numbers of support personnel, occasionally accompanied by their families, and extensive equipment, supply depots, airfields, barracks, and innumerable other facilities. Of course, there will be situations where such major operations are justified and necessary. But wherever this has been the case, there generally have been serious political problems, often leading to anti-American actions and perhaps lasting impairment of our relations with the people assisted by us. Such problems would be reduced if the objectives of our intervention can be achieved with the assistance of strategic airpower.

In addition to SAC's indirect limited-war role as a deterrent "umbrella" or "shield" which provides freedom of action, and its potential direct role in assuming the strategic phase of combat operations, SAC has another capability which is of vital importance to the *management* of crises and local conflicts, and that is global reconnaissance. In the first chapter I told of SAC's part in locating the missiles which the Soviets had placed on Cuba. As will be remembered, this operation furnished President Kennedy the photographic evidence on which he based his subsequent decisions and actions for achieving at least a temporary solution of the Cuban crisis.

Similar reconnaissance requirements exist in all situations where crises or local conflicts threaten to develop or are already in progress. Reconnaissance missions on the ground or even by short-range tactical aircraft can survey only relatively small areas and are often handicapped by political and other problems. However, SAC's specially equipped global reconnaissance aircraft can cover vast areas in a short period of time and can quickly discover and accurately locate any suspicious activities, installations or buildups. Also, SAC has the necessary organization, facilities and skilled personnel to rapidly process, evaluate and disseminate the intelligence gathered by its reconnaissance aircraft.

To appreciate the importance of global reconnaissance, it must be understood that, as a rule, the management of crises and limited wars entails perhaps 90 percent diplomatic action and only some 10 percent military action. But effective diplomatic action is contingent upon thorough and accurate intelligence regarding any potential aggressor's intentions and preparations or, in the event aggression is in progress, the extent and nature of the enemy's activities and deployment. All this requires extensive aerial surveillance and reconnaissance missions in many parts of the world. SAC has the capability to accomplish such missions on a global and continuing basis, because it had to establish that capability to carry out its primary mission of global strategic air operations.

In this discussion I have made little mention of the principal military forces for limited war and, instead, have emphasized the potential role of strategic airpower and, in particular, of the Strategic Air Command. I have done so for several reasons. For one, I am more familiar with the capabilities and operations of SAC. Next, the roles and missions of the conventional forces in limited war are well established and known while the employment of non-nuclear strategic airpower in this type of conflict has as yet been given little consideration. Finally, I am hopeful that better knowledge of the many potential advantages I described will lead to more extensive utilization of SAC's unique capabilities in future crises and limited wars.

I realize that there are objections to the use of SAC in local conflicts, for one reason or another. Perhaps the most difficult objection to answer is the argument that, as long as SAC bombers are employed, we may be tempted in an emergency to use them in their primary role—to deliver nuclear weapons. I believe there is a possibility that we may have to use such weapons in limited war under certain circumstances, but if this should ever become necessary, it would not result from the fact that SAC had been called in to drop conventional bombs. There are far more substantial reasons, and I think that a frank and factual discussion of the use of nuclear weapons in limited war may be appropriate at this point.

It is difficult to discuss this highly controversial subject factually because it involves emotions, the question of morals, and inconsistencies with respect to both. If the whole problem is one of relative morality in warfare, we should first examine the job of the military and, for that matter, the reasons which have brought the military into existence as one of man's oldest professions.

Putting aside all the fancy words and academic doubletalk, the basic reason for having a military is to do two jobs—to kill people and to destroy the works of man. To be sure, there are other jobs, such as defense against enemy attack and protection against aggression or, more sophisticated, deterrence of aggression. But to this day, the military has retained its basic two functions, and it trains its combat personnel to perform these two functions better than anyone else. Whatever other functions the military performs are essentially in support of the men whose job it is to kill and destroy.

We must keep this in mind when we try to decide on the morality of the weapons the military use, because what makes war immoral are not the weapons used to fight it but the objectives of the men who initiate wars to satisfy their greed and ambitions. Weapons are merely tools designed to extend the fighting strength of man, and they accomplish that purpose regardless of the cause they are serving. Thus, ever since man learned to use the club and spear as tools of combat, he has endeavored to develop weapons superior to those of his enemy and potent enough to compensate for any advantages the enemy might have.

History is replete with examples where new and "unconventional" weapons were decisive in bringing victory over a numerically superior or otherwise more powerful enemy equipped with "conventional" weapons. Perhaps the best known example is right in the Bible—the slingshot that brought little David victory over the giant Goliath who was armed with what was then a conventional weapon, a club. No one would question the morality of David's use of the slingshot, because it helped the good prevail over the evil.

While weapons grew ever more powerful and firepower grew ever more concentrated, the objectives of warfare remained the same; it just became costlier to pursue them. By the same token, the question of morality remained a relative concept because it was invariably the victor who decided which cause and weapons and strategy were moral—his own, needless to say. And regardless of any prevailing moral concepts, new weapons never remained "unconventional" for long because, in the eternal struggle for power and survival, nation after nation had to acquire and use these weapons until they became quite conventional—and moral. Actually, the moral objection to new weapons did not stem so much from the fact that they could kill more people; perhaps they killed no more people than the old weapons did, but they could do it in a shorter period of time, and that was what made them "immoral" in the minds of many people.

Then something happened far beyond the imagination of all people but a few—the development of nuclear weapons. Suddenly, it had become possible to pack into the bulk and weight of a blockbuster bomb of World War II—by now a conventional weapon—thousands and eventually millions of times more firepower. The world still has not recovered from the impact of this fantastic jump in concentrated firepower and all its implications.

It is, therefore, understandable that so many people consider the use of such a mass-killer weapon immoral. However, they forget that the now conventional—and presumably more moral—weapons of World War II caused an estimated 50 million-plus casualties and devastated many cities. If people are reminded of these grim statistics, they point out that it took some six years of fighting with conventional weapons to cause such casualties and devastation while nuclear weapons could do it all in a few hours. In other words, the difference between morality and immorality apparently lies in the time it takes to kill a given number of people and to destroy a given amount of the works of man.

Of course, this is an oversimplification of a very complex problem, and I am by no means trying to imply that I take the unparalleled destructiveness of nuclear weapons and their deadly side-effects lightly. But the point I am trying to make is that, throughout the thousands of years of the evolution of armaments, there has never been a weapon so revolutionary or "ultimate" that it failed to be surpassed by a still more revolutionary weapon and thus became conventional itself and, eventually, obsolete. By the same token, it would be folly to assume that nuclear weapons are the ultimate in firepower and that nuclear missiles are the ultimate weapon. In the years ahead, the ever accelerating pace of scientific advancement is bound to reach new plateaus of military technology which will make today's most advanced weapons seem crude and ineffective.

Long before this will come to pass, however, someone in this world will start using small nuclear munitions in a limited war —the Soviets or the Red Chinese or some little country or perhaps the United States. Other nations will follow suit until the nuclear weapon has become a conventional tool of warfare and a still more terrible weapon takes its place as the "unconventional"—and immoral—weapon of the day. All this is a frightening prospect to contemplate but we must be realistic and face the facts, however unpleasant. Most of all, we must realize that nuclear weapons will not go away simply because we want them to go away. No treaty or pact or ban can bring back pre-nuclear days nor can it make every dictator and aggressor tear up the secret of the hydrogen bomb.

It has been argued that it had been possible to ban the use of poison gas in World War II and that, as long as that ban had proved successful, a similar ban on the use of nuclear weapons should be similarly successful. But what made Hitler refrain from engaging in gas warfare was neither his respect for treaties nor moral issues; after all, he had proved his complete disrespect for treaties and utter lack of morality often and compellingly enough. The sole reason why Hitler did not resort to poison gas, even when the tide turned against him, was his realization that the disadvantages and problems associated with gas warfare greatly outweighed any military advantages he could expect. The opposite is true for nuclear weapons, at least under certain conditions.

Unless there should be an all-out nuclear war, the time will come eventually when some nation will resort to nuclear weapons in a limited war, because of necessity or to achieve a vital military objective. It is conceivable that *we* will be that nation. In some areas of local conflict we are and will be vastly outnumbered by the Communists. If we cannot overcome that disadvantage with our conventional forces and weapons, we may find ourselves in a situation where we have the choice of either sacrificing the lives of large numbers of our men or saving them through the use of nuclear munitions. I have little doubt that, in such a desperate situation, the President would authorize nuclear weapons and that he would be supported by the great majority of our citizens.

It almost came to such a decision in two major crises during the Korean war, once when our troops were trapped in the North by large hordes of Chinese and the other time when they were trapped in the "Pusan Perimeter." I happen to know how close we came to using atomic bombs to save our troops because, in both instances, I had been ordered to have SAC units stand by for such action.

There may be other unpredictable situations where we may have to use our best weapons in limited war in order to prevent grave impairment of our interests and security, and where we can no longer do so with the conventional forces at hand. It is, therefore, unrealistic to say that we will "never" use nuclear weapons in limited war. In fact, if we can convince our enemies that we are determined to do so if we have no other choice, they will make certain not to expand any limited conflict to the point where they would force us to employ nuclear munitions.

Apart from the issue of morality, the very possibility of using nuclear weapons in limited war immediately raises a number of other questions. The first pertains to the problem of how to control such use. Nuclear weapons in limited war—and I am speaking of small and "clean" weapons, that is, weapons which create little if any radiation—would either be dropped from aircraft or employed by special troops on the ground. I pre-viously described the extensive measures taken to prevent the inadvertent or unauthorized expenditure of nuclear weapons by SAC bomber crews. Similar measures would be used in lim-ited-war operations and would be just as reliable.

The nuclear munitions or "tactical nuclear weapons" which would be employed by ground troops, although of very low yield, are also subject to rigid controls and are, in my opinion, no less safe than the far more powerful missiles on Polaris submarines and the still more powerful SAC ICBMs in their underground silos. Having participated in the establishment of control procedures and having dealt, for many years, with com-bat crews who are entrusted with nuclear weapons, I am confident that the requirement for adequate control of such weapons, both in the air and on the ground, presents no major problem.

Another question concerns the danger of continuous increase in the size of the nuclear weapons we might use in limited war. The point is made that, once we start using nuclear weapons, however small they might be initially, we would be tempted to keep increasing the yield and, as a result, would precipitate an increase in the scope and intensity of the conflict which would be contrary to our stated limited-war policy. The answer to this argument is that the size or, more specifically, the yield of a nuclear weapon is always selected on the basis of the particular objective it is expected to achieve. It is highly unlikely that, in a limited war, any objective that would have to be accomplished with greater firepower than conventional weapons can provide, would require more than low-yield nuclear weapons.

This brings up a related question which pertains to the widespread concern that the use of any nuclear weapons in limited war would unavoidably lead to escalation into general nuclear war. It is argued that, if we start using nuclear munitions of any kind in a limited conflict, the Soviets and, more likely, the Red Chinese (once they have achieved a nuclear delivery capability) would counter with even bigger nuclear weapons so as to wrest the advantage from us. This, in turn, would compel us to increase the yield and number of our weapons as well as the scope of targets we would attack, and thus the conflict would expand rapidly and beyond control until we would be engaged in an all-out nuclear war, the very kind of war we are trying to deter.

I do not agree with this reasoning. In the first place, I believe that neither the Soviets nor the Red Chinese could risk escalation into general nuclear war as long as we possess a credible war-winning capability. Whenever they support or participate in a limited conflict, their objective is limited also, and it stands to reason that they would rather forego achievement of such a limited objective than risk getting into an all-out nuclear war which they cannot hope to win. Needless to say, we are equally anxious to prevent such a war. Therefore, it can be expected that diplomatic action—the major activity in any limited conflict—will bring a limited war in which nuclear weapons are used to an end before there is danger of uncontrollable escalation.

There is also another point. Even if the Soviets or, some years hence, the Red Chinese should ever feel confident enough to engage in a nuclear war with us, they would have to rely on a massive surprise attack so as to destroy our retaliatory capability to the greatest degree possible and thus keep the damage resulting from our counterattack to an acceptable minimum. The most unfavorable condition for them would be to get into a general nuclear war with us via a limited war because such a war serves as strategic warning of possible escalation. This warning gives us time to place all our nuclear strike forces on a status of complete and instant readiness, as was the case during the Cuban crisis. As a result, the Communists would be deprived of the most essential factor in their plans for nuclear aggression—the advantages of the initiative.

In discussing all these facets of the employment of nuclear weapons in limited war, I want to make it clear that I do *not* advocate the use of such weapons if it can be at all avoided. But it is conceivable that we may have no other choice, and we must be prepared for such a possibility. And if our national interests and security should ever make it essential to use nuclear weapons in a local war, none of the popular concerns and objections appear valid enough to prevent us from doing so.

There is, of course, far more to the problems of limited war than the issues which I covered above. I used these issues to support my contention that we have the means and the capability to counter every phase of the Communist offensive, provided we make effective use of the full potential inherent in each of our diverse forces and make certain that they always complement one another in serving the common objective. As long as we do so, I am confident we will go a long way toward managing the perplexing problems of Communist-led crises and limited wars.

Still, this is only part of the overall problem of fighting the Communist conspiracy. We cannot cure the ills of the world by curing local symptoms but only by combating the very cause that is producing all these symptoms. From our point of view, it makes little difference whether the Communists try to reach their goal in many small steps or a few big steps or one very big step. We can keep them from taking any of these steps only so long as we make it unmistakably clear to them that we are resolved not to let them go any farther. And therein lies the whole secret of managing limited wars.

11. Deterrence and Space

IN June 1957 I spoke to an engineering society in Los Angeles on the Air Force's effort in space technology. I was still the head of the Air Research and Development Command but slated to return to SAC the following month and succeed General Curtis E. LeMay as Commander in Chief. Therefore, the industrialists and engineers in my audience expected me to discuss the military potential of space, both from a technological and operational point of view. But I had to disappoint them.

Guided by official policy, I carefully avoided any references to satellites, space vehicles and man in space. Instead, I talked about the Air Force's high-altitude studies, the impact of solar phenomena on communications, and related subjects. The reason which prevented me from speaking more freely was that, in those days, it was considered "inappropriate" for an officer in a responsible position to venture into an area which was the acknowledged realm of research scientists and fiction writers.

Less than four months later the space age dawned upon us with a blast—the blast that lofted the first Russian Sputnik into orbit.

Today, we may be amused about the unrealistic attitude toward space that prevailed in this country at that time. But I think that we have little reason to be amused because, in at least one important respect, the attitude toward space is still quite unrealistic. To be sure, the word "space" has at last attained respectability, and there is hardly an official speech or article which does not refer to the "challenge of space." Nevertheless, there are many people who insist that space must be used for peaceful purposes only and, therefore, strongly oppose any plans for the military use of space.

I consider this attitude unrealistic because the people who frown on the military use of space fail to understand that space is merely an operating medium like land and sea, not a tool or weapon in itself. To them, space is something tangible that begins at a given number of miles above their door step and is marked off by a fence to which they can attach a No TRESPASSING sign. Unfortunately, no one would respect such a "sign," least of all our enemies.

In reality, space begins at the very surface of the earth, with a rapidly thinning blanket of air for the first few miles. If we were to mark a border between "our air" and "everybody's space," it would have to be entirely arbitrary because there is no natural dividing line between "territorial" and "international" air or space. Hence, the word "aerospace" was coined to designate all of the vast realm that begins at the surface of the earth and stretches to the farthest reaches of the universe. And whether we like it or not, there is no way to make any part of aerospace off-limits for military operations.

Ever since the military balloon and, later, the airplane added a third dimension to warfare, man has endeavored to go higher and higher in following the traditional military mandate of "seeking the high ground." Some of our aircraft already have reached altitudes which, for all practical purposes, can be considered space. And today's ballistic missiles, which curve to altitudes of hundreds of miles in their trajectory, do in fact use space as an operating medium. Where we spoke of "altitude above sea level," we are now speaking of "distance from the earth," and no one can predict how high or to what distance from the earth some nation or nations will try to go in the endeavor to gain a military advantage.

It is still too early to do more than speculate about the potentials of military operations in space, just as it would have been impossible a few decades ago to foresee the impact of the airplane on military tactics and strategy. But there can be no doubt that the possibilities of military space operations are indeed staggering. It would, therefore, be folly to assume that the Soviets would fail to recognize these possibilities and would hesitate to exploit them for both their political and military ends.

Under these circumstances, I am convinced that we have no other choice but to take whatever precautionary measures may be needed to protect ourselves against any threat from or in space, despite our desire to reserve space for peaceful pursuits. The considerations that must guide us in this respect were summed up pointedly by John F. Kennedy when, as a senator, he said: "Control of space will be decided in the next decade. If the Soviets control space, they can control the earth." This means that it is not enough for us to merely keep up with the Soviets. We must surpass them in every phase of the space effort so as to prevent them from gaining control of space, denying us the space medium, and using space for aggressive purposes.

It should, therefore, be evident that the achievement of superiority in space is not merely a matter of scientific pride and national prestige to us but essential to the future welfare and security of the Free World. Our government has made it clear that this requires a military space capability. As President Lyndon B. Johnson declared when he was still the Vice-President: "The present world situation allows us no choice. We must have a military as well as a civilian space capability."

Some people claim to see an inconsistency in the fact that this country exhibits an interest in military space applications while, at the same time, professing its desire to ensure the peaceful use of the space medium. But there is no inconsistency at all because there can be no more peaceful endeavor than to make sure that, to quote President Kennedy again, "no nation secure a position in space which can threaten the security of the United States and the Free World."

It should be emphasized that any military space capability which we may develop would not be directed against any particular nation, such as the Soviet Union or Red China. It would be directed against any potential aggressor who, at some time in the future, might pose an offensive threat in space or attempt to deny us the space medium for peaceful pursuits. I submit that this concern on our part is well warranted. Just as we are now witnessing a gradual proliferation of nuclear capability, there is the distinct possibility of future proliferation of space capability. This would enable a growing number of countries to use space for aggressive purposes unless we are in a position to prevent them effectively from doing so.

For all these reasons, our military space effort is essentially a matter of self-defense which is the right and duty of all sovereign nations, and especially of this country as the Free World's principal bulwark against Communist aggression. But a review of the work done in this area so far shows that little has been accomplished that would promise any kind of military space capability within the foreseeable future. It is true that the progress made in communications and weather satellites, although designed primarily for civilian purposes, will benefit military operations also. What concerns me, however, is the lack of similar progress in purely military space applications which would serve to maintain our deterrent strength in the face of any future threat from space. Perhaps our main problem in this respect stems from the fact that we cannot predict the exact nature of the threat which we may have to meet.

It has been said that military space technology is now at the stage where aerial warfare was in 1908 when the War Department accepted its first airplane from the Wright Brothers. I would go further than that and say that it is at the stage of the very beginnings of the military utilization of air, namely, the French Revolution in the eighteenth century when balloons were first used for battlefield observation. Then as now, no one could predict the ultimate potential of the new operating medium, let alone speculate on how best to exploit that potential—or how an enemy might exploit it.

But despite the many unknowns and variables with which we have to deal, we cannot afford to wait until the threat materializes and we know enough about it to start figuring out what to do about it. For, by then, we would be so far behind technologically and militarily that we would never be able to counter whatever the threat may be and might well find ourselves at the mercy of the aggressor. In this dilemma, we have the choice of three different approaches we can pursue.

The first approach requires that we try to anticipate, as best we can, the general nature of any military threat from or in space we may have to face, both in the immediate and more distant future, and then develop countermeasures which would permit a wide range of applications. I call this the "defensive approach."

The second approach entails the expeditious development of a space weapon system which would complement our present retaliatory forces and thus lend added and lasting strength to our deterrent. This might be called the "deterrent approach."

The third approach is based on the argument that, while we have made great strides in space technology, we still know too little about future space potentials to establish parameters for an operational capability in either the defensive or offensive areas. Therefore, the proponents of this approach maintain that we should direct our military space effort primarily toward basic research in all the scientific disciplines and fields which, in one way or another, can contribute to the development of military space systems, both manned and unmanned. Thus, by the time we can determine definite operational requirements for such systems, we would have the knowledge and techniques or, in other words, the "building blocks" to develop them speedily and economically.

The choice among these three approaches is not only a most difficult one but also very critical because we cannot afford to make a mistake. If this country should suddenly be confronted with a "space Cuba" and have the wrong or perhaps no means to deal with such an emergency, our very survival might be at stake.

What makes the choice so difficult is a complex combination of a variety of factors, such as political considerations, limitations of resources and technological problems. It must also be borne in mind that the lead time required to bring a new weapon system from original inception to operational readiness, which normally takes years, can be expected to be considerably longer for military space systems even if we should have all the essential "building blocks." Furthermore, the state of the art advances at such a rapid pace that any space system under development may be obsolete before it becomes operational and, hence, may no longer suffice to cope with the more up-to-date weapon systems an aggressor may produce.

In my opinion, none of the above-mentioned approaches—the defensive, deterrent and "building block" approaches—will by itself suffice to counter the overall threat from space. Some phases of that threat may lie in the distant future and would justify the "building block" approach. But other phases may well materialize very unexpectedly, in the immediate or near future. Therefore, we should select that combination of all three approaches which makes the most economic use of our human and material resources on one hand and, on the other, promises an adequate military space capability for both the immediate and distant future.

I am confident that this can be accomplished through continued close cooperation between the Department of Defense and the National Aeronautics and Space Administration (NASA) which has the responsibility for the civilian space effort. In this effort, the NASA has had considerable assistance from the military and, in turn, can help the military space effort by creating the "building blocks" that are to enhance the development of future military space systems. This would leave the military free to concentrate on the more immediate space needs, that is, early defensive and deterrent or offensive space systems as well as certain types of support systems.

I believe that military requirements in these three areas are well enough defined to warrant the development of several space systems, both unmanned and manned, which would greatly contribute to our security and the preservation of our deterrent. The most urgently needed military space system, in my opinion, is a reconnaissance satellite which would permit continuous surveillance of all hostile areas in the world. A small number of reconnaissance satellites in appropriate orbits is an ideal means for providing timely and comprehensive information such as we need for accurate assessment of the global threat to our survival.

There is also a requirement for satellites to detect the launching of ballistic missiles. As I pointed out earlier, the Ballistic Missile Early Warning System (BMEWS) now in existence will provide us the 15 to 20 minutes' warning of a Soviet missile attack which suffices to get SAC's ground-alert forces airborne. But the BMEWS radars can detect only those missiles that streak in from the north and provide no warning against missiles approaching from the south or fired by submarines off our coasts.

Therefore, the challenge is to develop a system which would provide *omnidirectional* warning as well as the longest possible warning time by detecting the firing of any missiles immediately or shortly upon launch. Considerable work has been done on an unmanned space system which may accomplish this purpose. But whether the ultimate solution will be offered by a space system or a land-based system which, as President Johnson announced in September 1964, uses "over the horizon" radars, there can be no doubt that the assurance of omnidirectional and timely warning against a missile attack is indispensable to the preservation of a credible deterrent.

Another urgent requirement is defense against a military threat from space. This requirement is more difficult to meet because, as I indicated before, we cannot predict, with any degree of assurance, the nature of the threat against which we may have to defend ourselves in the future. As we are in a retaliatory role, it is entirely up to the aggressor to decide, not only when and where to strike, but also what means and strategies to employ. To exploit the advantages inherent in the initiative, an aggressor would make the fullest use of the element of surprise. This would apply to the timing of the attack as well as to the employment of some radically new weapon or technique for which we are not prepared. It is quite possible that the Soviets' surprise weapon would be an offensive space system but, beyond this assumption, we can only speculate.

Our problem is further aggravated by the fact that the Soviets have cloaked their space efforts in the utmost secrecy which, of course, is far easier in their type of police state than in an open society such as ours. As a result, we have heard nothing about their military space programs except occasional boasts which, although of a very general nature, are rather indicative of their intentions. We do know, however, that the Soviets possess considerable competence in three areas which could contribute to a variety of offensive space systems. These areas are: powerful boosters which make it possible to loft large payloads into orbit; advanced guidance systems which would permit accurate target coverage from space; nuclear weapons with several times the yield of our largest weapons.

It is, therefore, within the Soviets' capability to produce space systems, either manned or unmanned, which could carry high-yield nuclear weapons and, through the unprecedented threat they pose, would gravely impair our deterrent. For instance, it is conceivable that we may wake up one morning and find a number of Soviet satellites floating in stationary orbits over every part of the United States. If the Soviets would inform us that these satellites carried multi-megaton nuclear weapons which could be released upon radio command from Russia, they would be in a strong position to blackmail us into any concession they might demand.

We certainly must anticipate such a contingency, which is by no means farfetched or far in the future, and make sure that we have *operational* defensive systems or measures to cope with it. I would not presume to say whether one or both of the satellite defense systems, which were also announced by President Johnson in September 1964, can meet all future needs. However, I believe that, eventually, a space defense system capable of dealing with any kind of hostile space vehicle would require a manned and maneuverable "space interceptor." Assisted by missile-warning satellites, such "interceptors" may well have the added capability of destroying enemy ballistic missiles far from their intended targets.

Related to the requirement for space defense systems is the need to develop means for the inspection of suspicious satellites. A large number of manmade objects are now orbiting the earth. In addition to instrumented satellites launched by both ourselves and the Soviets, there is also considerable space debris, that is, components of the rockets employed to put the satellites in orbit. Because of the steadily growing number and small size of all these objects it will become increasingly difficult to keep track of them, let alone determine their nature.

Future developments may permit conclusive inspection of potentially hostile satellites and, if need be, their neutralization from the ground or by means of some type of unmanned space vehicle. However, it would appear more feasible to use maneuverable spacecraft, manned by crews who can search out suspected weapons carriers, board them and, if required, destroy them. Perhaps the above-mentioned "space interceptors" could be designed to perform this added function.

Looking still farther into the future, there may be the requirement for a spaceborne command post which, in an emergency, could assume command and control of our global strike forces. As I pointed out in my discussion of SAC's airborne command post, effective command and control of our strike forces is an integral component of our overall retaliatory capability, and its survivability in case of a surprise attack is, therefore, a vital element of a credible deterrent. SAC's airborne command post, in conjunction with its global communications network, provides a highly survivable emergency means for the centralized command and control of SAC's worldwide strike forces. But execution of the Single Integrated Operational Plan for all the nation's nuclear strike forces—underwater, on the ground, in the air and, perhaps, in space—eventually may require still more centralized control. And future developments in weapons may demand further improvements in survivability. A joint spaceborne command post, staffed by competent officers from all services and carrying complete communications equipment, could probably meet these conditions.

Finally, we must give some thought to any future need for a space weapon system, a manned or unmanned vehicle for space-to-ground offense. It is true that, as a nation, we abhor the very prospect of offensive weapons in space, and if it were possible to conclude enforceable international treaties for banning "weapons of mass destruction" in space, we would no doubt take the lead in promoting such treaties. On the other hand, we must be realistic enough to accept the fact that, regardless of any future treaties, some aggressive nation may succeed in placing offensive weapons in space. To prevent any nation from thus gaining control of space, we may have no choice but to counter with an offensive space capability of our own.

I am confident that, if our survival should demand extension of our strategic capability into space, this nation will be ready and willing to do so. This may require the addition of manned strategic spacecraft to SAC's inventory, permitting a continuous spaceborne alert. If this should materialize, SAC someday may have a truly mixed force of bombers, missiles and spacecraft which, in my opinion, would be the most promising safeguard for peace in the space age.

The various military space systems which I described above should make it clear that, despite all the uncertainty and variables, there are many things we can do and some things we must do in order to protect ourselves against any future threat from space. Ever since the need for a military space capability became apparent, I have urged a vigorous program for the pursuit of space projects which I considered of the greatest importance to SAC. Although we have expended a considerable effort on space programs, it has been mainly in support of the civilian-oriented projects of the National Aeronautics and Space Administration. What we need is a more vigorous *military* space effort.

As we plan for the future, we must realize that our design for survival never ends, but that there is always a new chapter with a new threat and a new challenge. And the new chapter on space has plenty of both.

12. The Ultimate Weapon

THERE is much talk these days about the ever growing role of "electronic brains" and automation, not only in business and industry but also in the military. In fact, many people seem to think that the nuclear-tipped ballistic missile is the "Ultimate Weapon" and that it has brought about "push-button warfare" which leaves little else for the military man to do besides figuring out what buttons to push and when.

But all the electronic brains in the world cannot take the place of the human mind and brain when we are dealing with intangibles that cannot be keyed into a computer. There never has been and there never will be a mechanical substitute for man's ingenuity, devotion and courage. Yet these are the very qualities on which the deterrent strength of our nation is founded.

In discussing the military aspects of deterrence, I have dwelled on the strategies, the tools and many other factors that are of concern to our Deterrent System. But I have made only passing references to the human element and, hence, there remains one final and, in my opinion, the most important factor to be discussed—the men and the people who make deterrence work.

Perhaps we have become so enamored with machines that we

are prone to give them more credit than they deserve. We never speak of a hammer that built a house or a typewriter that wrote a book or a brush that painted a house. But we do not hesitate to speak of computers that can do the thinking of a hundred men and of black boxes that guide airplanes and of bombs that can kill millions of people. We forget that it is not the computer or black box or bomb that thinks or guides or kills but man who has conceived and uses these tools.

Modern tools and weapons can perform extraordinary feats but, while they may be able to achieve the improbable, only man can achieve the impossible. Indeed, man is at once the most useful of all tools and the most destructive of all weapons. In the truest sense of the word, none other than man himself is the Ultimate Weapon. We should bear these thoughts in mind as we try to appraise the effectiveness of our deterrent and contemplate the things we must do to maintain it.

The point is that many of our citizens are inclined to feel secure as long as we have the best and the most weapons in the world. But they tend to overlook two facts. First, even the best strategies we can devise and the most advanced weapons we can produce have little deterrent value unless we have also the best military men to carry out these strategies and to handle these weapons. And, second, the military deterrent is only one phase of our defense against the Communist offensive and only one part of the Deterrent System against the Communist conspiracy. All other phases and parts are the responsibility of both the individual citizen and the American people as a whole.

Let me speak first of some problems regarding the overall quality of the men in our armed forces. As weapon systems become ever more complex and destructive, the men who control, operate and maintain these weapon systems must possess personal and professional qualifications far superior to those ever demanded of military men in the past. This may seem self-understood but I have often had the impression that there is greater concern for the quality and care of the weapon systems and equipment than for the quality and care of the men entrusted with them.

We are devoting a sizable share of our economic, scientific and industrial resources to the development and production of military matériel of the highest quality, but we do not do nearly enough to make certain that the overall quality of our military personnel is just as high. We insist on "cost effectiveness" to get more military *power* per dollar, but we seem to forget that it is equally important to get more military *man* per dollar. We are spending billions of dollars to teach men the advanced skills required in modern warfare, but we do not expend a commensurate effort to keep these men in the service so that the taxpayers get a fair return for their investment.

I believe it is essential that we make a determined effort to raise the overall quality of our military personnel so that it matches the quality of our weapons, because both together establish the quality of our military deterrent. In my opinion, the best way to achieve the standards of quality we will need in the critical times ahead is through a truly *professional* force that offers the prestige and inducements to attract and retain men of the highest caliber.

We have such men in the armed forces now, despite the fact that men with their qualifications and skills normally could do far better in civilian life. There are the graduates of the service academies who provide many of our finest officers. There are the officers and men, both regulars and reserves, who have made the military their career because they like it and want to contribute their share to the nation's defense. Often, this entails considerable sacrifices, not only on the part of the men but also of their families. I told of SAC's combat crews who must spend much of their time on alert away from their homes. This is true also for the crews of the Polaris submarines who spend many weeks on patrol duty, and for many others of our fighting men. We are fortunate to have such men because their professionalism and dedication lend substance to the deterrent potential of the weapon systems they man.

But there are also men in uniform who contribute little if anything to the overall deterrent. Some, who serve their obligated tour, do so without enthusiasm and are just waiting to get back into civilian life. Others stay in the service merely because they cannot do better in civilian life and, often, are nothing but deadwood. And there are some who manage to get into the service although they lack the moral and other qualities to make them useful members of the military team. In fact, there have been judges who have given young lawbreakers the choice of going to jail or joining the armed forces, as if the military service were an institution for the rehabilitation of delinquents and misfits. On the other hand, there are highly qualified career reservists who should and want to be retained on active duty but who must be retired after twenty years of service to permit adequate "career progression" for younger officers.

Many of these problems could be resolved if the military would gradually be converted to a professional force. This could be achieved, for instance, if all men entering the military service, except graduates of the service academies, would have to serve in a probationary status for a given number of years. By the time they complete their probationary tour, they certainly will know whether or not they desire a professional military career. Of those who do, the best qualified should be selected for retention and given "regular" status.

Other qualified men who prefer civilian careers but want to continue serving their country should be given the opportunity to join the reserves or National Guard so that they are ready to augment the regular establishment whenever the need arises. Thus, there would no longer be a distinction between the "career reservist" and the "regular" because all men who can be retained on active duty would be regulars. At the same time, the reserves and National Guard would be strengthened by the addition of men who have had several years of active military experience and have proved to be of high quality.

Such a system would result not only in raising the overall quality of our military personnel but also in great savings. By eliminating the deadwood and misfits, total numbers can be reduced considerably without affecting fighting strength in any way. The investment in training would yield far greater returns, and overall training cost would decrease.

Some of the moneys thus saved could be used to increase the pay and benefits for the military professionals. This would help attract more young men to the military career which, in turn, would permit greater selectivity. To further enhance the attractiveness—and quality—of the military, every effort should be made to gain for it the prestige it deserves as a vital and demanding profession. This applies not only to the officers but also to the noncommissioned officers who often are the key to the success of a military unit if given the proper authority and standing.

Throughout my military career, I have worked with men of all branches, all ranks and all types, both in war and peace. On the basis of my experiences, I am convinced that only a professional peacetime force such as I outlined can provide the consistently high quality of military personnel which, in combination with the high quality of our weapons, will assure the preservation of our military superiority.

But while it takes military superiority to *win* wars, it takes far more to *prevent* wars. Military strength for war becomes political strength for peace only when it is supported by the sum total of every deterrent inherent in a strong and united nation. For deterrence is more than bombs and missiles and tanks and armies.

Deterrence is a sound economy and prosperous industry. Deterrence is scientific progress and good schools. Deterrence is effective civil defense and the maintenance of law and order. Deterrence is the practice of religion and respect for the rights and convictions of others. Deterrence is a high standard of morals and wholesome family life. Deterrence is honesty in public office and freedom of the press. Deterrence is all these things and many more, for only a nation that is healthy and strong in every respect has the power and will to deter the forces from within and without that threaten its survival.

We excel in some of these things but in others we are quite deficient. It is not within my province to belabor these deficiencies and propose solutions. There are others, far better qualified, who are devoting their lives to these problems. But here again, there is no mechanical or electronic substitute for the initiative and dedication of the men on whom we depend to resolve the nation's problems. And there is no substitute for the wisdom and judgment of the nation's elected leaders in making the best possible use of all our tools of deterrence.

Still, the ultimate weapon in our design for survival are the American people, individually and collectively. They must be made to understand that, in the nuclear age, the primary mission of the military is no longer to win wars but to help deter them, and that the military can no longer do its job alone. It must be impressed on every citizen that he or she is a soldier in the battle for survival, because that battle must be waged on many fronts in addition to the military front and must be fought with many weapons in addition to military weapons.

That is why, throughout these pages, I have emphasized again and again that the American people must be made aware of the threat to our survival and kept informed of the problems and issues this threat entails. Being a military man, I have discussed primarily those issues which have a bearing on the military phase of our Deterrent System. But since the military threat to our survival is the most ominous one, I believe that these are the issues which are of the most immediate concern to my fellow citizens.

Many people may disagree with some or all of my ideas and conclusions and recommendations. But it really does not matter whether they agree or not. If this book accomplishes nothing more than to stimulate wider discussion of the very pressing and complex issues before us, it will have served its purpose. Far-reaching decisions will have to be made, and the public must know every aspect of the issues involved so that, through intelligent and thorough discussion, the most feasible and promising solutions can be found. That is democracy in action.

And so, as I look to the future, I see much reason for concern but also for confidence. I am concerned because I am not convinced that there is sufficient recognition of the nature and gravity of the threat to our security and welfare. Still I am confident that we can meet this threat, as we have met the threats of the past, as long as our citizens maintain their inflexible determination to survive as a people and prevail as a nation.